The
Philosophical
Programmer

The Philosophical Programmer

REFLECTIONS ON THE MOTH IN THE MACHINE

Daniel Kohanski

ST. MARTIN'S PRESS
New York

Intel™ and Pentium® are trademarks of Intel Corporation. VAX is a trademark of Digital Equipment Corporation. MS-DOS, Windows 95, and Windows NT are trademarks of Microsoft. JAVA is a trademark of Sun Microsystems. MVS and TSO are trademarks of IBM. Unicode® is a trademark of Unicode, Inc.

Library of Congress Cataloging-In-Publication Data

Kohanski, Daniel.
    The philosophical programmer : reflections on the moth in the machine / Daniel Kohanski. — 1st ed.
        p.   cm.
    Includes bibliographical references.
    ISBN 0-312-18650-9
    1. Electronic digital computers — Programming — Philosophy.
    I. Title.
    QA76.6.K6445   1998
    005.1'01 — dc21   98-9792
                                                                    CIP

Book design by Jenny Dossin

First Edition: July 1998

10 9 8 7 6 5 4 3 2

Insofar as the laws of mathematics refer to reality, they are not certain. And insofar as they are certain, they do not refer to reality.

Albert Einstein

In the design of programming languages one can let oneself be guided primarily by considering "what the machine can do." Considering, however, that the programming language is the bridge between the user and the machine—that it can, in fact, be regarded as his tool—it seems just as important to take into consideration "what Man can think."

Edsger W. Dijkstra

For Jean

And for Pat, who should have lived to see this.

Contents

Preface

In less than three generations, the computer has gone from being a scientific curiosity and military secret to becoming the defining technology of the age. In the last fifteen years alone, its status has changed from the prized possession of a university or corporation to that of a common household appliance—and one that is sometimes replaced every year or two as new developments make the current one obsolete. In the last five years, books have flooded the marketplace describing in detail what some computer product does, or how to write programs in some particular language on some specific machine. Yet there has been very little discussion about what programming *is* and about the meaning of programs for our lives.

This book tries to look at that question, and to look at it from a philosophical perspective. The starting point for any philosophical inquiry, particularly in the modern age, is from the standpoint of humanity: What is the impact of programming on the human beings who write programs, who use programs, and who in some way are affected by what programmers do? Another approach is to look for common structures in our activities; applied to programming, such an inquiry examines what a program is and how it is put together, and what principles of construction we can discover through this examination.

To do this, I have looked at programming and computers not only as they are now but as they used to be. We build upon the past, and the computer's past—short as it is—explains much about the way we have come to work with it today. The conventions of programming are by no means intuitive, and they are as much the result of accidents of history as they are the product of deliberate design. Understanding how the conventions developed will help us to remember them when intuition fails.

So, although this is not a "how-to" book and will not teach anyone how to write a program, it will look into what the writing of programs is all about. As such, I hope it will be useful to beginning programmers who need a solid foundation on which to start construction, as well as to my more experienced colleagues in the field, who will benefit from a review of skills that can sometimes become too much a matter of rote.

Most of this book is also for the general reader, someone who wants an idea of what computers are and what programmers do, and why we do it this way. Some chapters are necessarily more technical than others, and I have tried to organize them so that the beginning parts of each will give a general idea of what is going on. A nontechnical reader can skim through the rest of the chapter with no real loss of the sense of the whole.

The first part of the book, then, is a philosophical introduction to computers and programming; that is, it explores what a computer is and what its impact is, and discusses some of the problems that it poses for those who must master its intricacies. The second part describes how the computer is seen by the programmer, while the third goes into some detail about the tools that programmers use. The final part, again a philosophical inquiry, looks at the problems and opportunities the computer offers to humanity as a whole.

The
Philosophical
Programmer

Part I

A

PHILOSOPHICAL

INTRODUCTION

1

BEYOND THE CUCKOO CLOCK

The degree to which we make and use tools is one of the qualities that distinguishes us from the rest of the animal kingdom. Even so simple a thing as a pointed rock gave our hominid ancestors new powers: They could use it to cut up meat, and could even kill game that had previously been too strong, too fast, or simply too big for their unaided bodies to handle. A dead limb might become a lever to pry up a boulder that their muscles by themselves could never budge. The essence of a tool is that it extends our reach, multiplies the power of our limbs, improves our eyesight, and in countless other ways increases our ability to manipulate and control the world around us. The development of new tools is one of the ways in which we measure the progress of our species from hominid to human.

Until recently (that is, recently even by historical standards), tools were used primarily to extend the physical powers of our bodies. We use the hammer to increase the power of our fist; we use the plow to help break up soil too hard for our fingers; we use sacks to carry more seed than our hands can hold. All of these require our physical presence and our physical involvement, and for all of them, no matter how much they magnify the power of our muscles, they are limited to providing an incremental increase of the enabling muscle power.

Now consider an example of a different kind of tool: the medieval clock. It was driven not by the constant action of our muscles but by the movement of weights and counterweights; once set in motion, it could function for hours or days with no further human intervention. Whereas other tools altered our environment, the clock altered our perception of the environment instead. Much of this was done deliberately; monks in their medieval monasteries had committed themselves to saying their prayers at precisely defined times of the day, and to miss even once was to put their immortal souls in peril. Rather than guess at the hour of Prime (6 A.M.), they developed ever more sophisticated instruments to announce the time for them. Thus they left the natural time of circadian rhythm and daily course of the sun, choosing instead to be guided by instruments which they had devised but over which they had somewhat less than complete control—for of course they could not arbitrarily change the time once it had been established. In a small way, this tool exerted control over the toolmaker.

Because tools such as the clock expand the power of our minds rather than our muscles, it becomes part of their function to give us guidance and even control. The human mind cannot measure time with the accuracy of even a cuckoo clock, so we have learned to rely on timepieces to determine the proper time and will even cite them as authority for our actions. When the cuckoo comes out to sound the hour, we assume that it is correct. That is to say, we depend on the clockmaker's skill to provide us with an accurate device. And as with other tools of this sort, as their complexity increases it becomes harder and harder for the ordinary, unskilled user to fix them when they go wrong, or sometimes even to be aware that they have gone wrong at all.

The modern computer is even more a tool of the mind than is the cuckoo clock. Although its appendages can manipulate physical objects with great precision and dexterity, the computer itself is essentially a tool that extends the power of our thoughts. But it goes far beyond the cuckoo clock and any other mind tool we have invented thus far because, unlike any of them, it is a general-purpose tool that can be transformed almost at whim into nearly anything that our minds can conceive.

Yet there are still some ways in which the cuckoo clock resembles the computer. It processes raw data—the movement of weights or a spring or a pendulum—into useful information: the time. Once started and set, it operates for the most part without human intervention. It makes decisions, such as when to send the cuckoo out to sound the hour, on its own, again without human intervention once the clockmaker has designed and built its gears. The cuckoo clock and its contemporaries are in fact early examples of what today would be called an analog computer.

Analogs are representations of objects in the world. An analog computer processes these representations as continuous streams of information—a flow rather than a set of discrete intervals. It is the difference between a sweep second hand and one that jumps from second to second; the sweep movement is an exact analog of all the infinite instants of time. What makes the cuckoo clock a kind of analog computer is its processing of the continuous swings of its pendulum or the smooth rise and fall of its weight and counterweight.

Analog computers are not widely used these days. While they can handle infinitely varied input, they are limited in their ability to preserve and manipulate this data. A telephone circuit can carry the nuances and tones of a human voice in all its infinite varieties, but as the voice travels from switch to switch on its way to its destination, it loses more and more of its quality until, sent far enough, it can become unrecognizable gibberish. The power of the modern computer comes in large part from its processing of data as a set of discrete units — as digital information. Digital technology analyzes the continuous voice curve and assigns a number to various points on the curve. These numbers are then transmitted to the receiving end, which reconverts them into sounds that, while not a perfect match for the original, provide a close approximation. Digital technology trades perfect representation of the original data for a perfect preservation of the representation. To return to our clock example, an analog clock may use a sweep second hand which might be exactly accurate, but which cannot be exactly described. On the other hand, one can look at the face of a modern digital timepiece and describe exactly what time it reads, though such a clock is accurate, at best, only to the nearest second.

Digital technology provides far more flexibility in toolmaking than the analog world can. The cuckoo clock can decide when to send out the cuckoo, but that is about it. The microcomputer in a modern answering machine, however, can tell us what time a call came in, how long the message ran, and perhaps even where it came from. In theory, we could build an analog device to do these things as well. But it would not be able to do anything else unless we disassembled it and rebuilt it for its new task. The digital computer, however, uses for its instructions a set of discrete numbers rather than a series of gears or other analog devices. Thus the advantage of the digital computer is that to change what it does, we need only change these instruction numbers—its programming—and start it up again. If we want to add new features to the answering machine, in many cases we can do so simply by reprogramming it.

It is this idea of programming that gives the modern computer its power. Merely by changing a set of written instructions we create new tools out of the same physical device: we can turn the computer into a clock, an adding machine, a typewriter, or even a chess or Scrabble player. For the first time, words themselves have become tools which *in and of themselves* cause things to happen. Manual dexterity need no longer be a requirement for a physical creation; instead, it is the ingenuity of the programmer's thinking that is crucial to bringing an idea to fruition. In this new era, the primary creative force is becoming less and less the hand and more and more the word.

Words—instructions to a computer—have become tools largely because of another major component of the modern computer: its memory. Early computing devices were driven by numbers punched as holes in cards or paper tape; even today, a Jacquard loom will weave a cloth pattern as directed by a punched card, and player pianos will play music according to the notches on a drum. The Harvard Mark I, which started operation in 1944, followed instructions punched on holes in paper tape to produce gunnery tables for the U.S. Navy. All such devices, however, had a common limitation: they could not change the instructions or the data on their own. If any change was needed—a new formula for a table, for example—the entire tape had to be punched all over again.

By the time the Mark I was running, engineers had already recognized this restriction and were working to overcome it by developing methods of storing numbers in a modifiable medium — that is, memory. Early forms of memory included mercury delay lines, vacuum tubes, and magnetic drums. The ENIAC, another prototype computer built during World War II, used 18,000 vacuum tubes — a phenomenal number for the time. By 1954, core memories — small doughnut-shaped magnets on a wire grid — were in use in commercial computers, and the transistor was replacing the vacuum tube. It was now possible to store large groups of numbers that could be easily manipulated at electronic speed.

The EDVAC project, successor to the ENIAC, inspired another breakthrough, one that now defines the modern computer: *the idea of a program as data*. The ENIAC was programmed, as some of its predecessors had been, by setting wire plugs in a board. This method not only made reprogramming a time-consuming chore, but it also made programs slow to execute. The mathematician John von Neumann, assisting the ENIAC and EDVAC projects in 1944–45, documented a new approach that has since been likened to the invention of the wheel: storing the instructions in the computer's memory along with the data.[†]

†Who to credit for the concept of the stored-program computer is the subject of a long-running historical argument. Von Neumann sometimes gets sole credit, largely because he wrote the first (and only) draft of the paper describing the theoretical principles of the EDVAC design and is listed as its sole author. Some historians, however, believe that credit should be shared by the members of the EDVAC team, in particular Herman Goldstine, John Mauchly, Presper Eckert, and Arthur Burks (Campbell-Kelly and Aspray 1996, 94–95; Stern 1981, 76–77). Tensions between von Neumann and Eckert and Mauchly may also have contributed to the controversy (Stern 1981, 74–82). It is also possible that the British mathematician Alan Turing came up with the idea first; evidently he was one of the first to explain it in print (Ritchie 1986, 103, 177–79). Whatever the true story may be, stored-program computers are even today known as "von Neumann machines."

Storing the program in memory meant that the new computer could access each instruction at the same electronic speed with which it accessed the data. But it also meant that the computer could treat instructions as though they were themselves data — that is, numbers to be manipulated. This ability is the basis of all modern programming. A programmer writes a program — a set of instructions — using words that more or less resemble English (or other natural language) and enters these words into the computer as data. A program called a *compiler* then examines these words and converts them into numeric instructions, which the computer circuitry can execute. It then puts these new numbers into memory, and the computer executes them. A program can even alter its own instructions in response to changing circumstances, which is a basic prerequisite of artificial intelligence. Just as we change and refine our actions as we learn more about our environment, so the computer is capable of altering its programming as it acquires more data.

Each instruction that the computer executes is stored in a particular location in its memory, and the computer normally proceeds from one instruction to the next. However, there are some instructions which will alter the flow of execution based on some condition — for instance, if the value of a piece of data exceeds a defined threshold, the computer will be directed to execute a different set of instructions than it would have otherwise. These types of instructions are called *conditional branch instructions,* and they give the computer the ability to make decisions. In a rocket guidance system, for example, the computer is constantly receiving new data — the current position, speed, and angle — and making decisions based on that data to increase or decrease the fuel flow to the various thrusters that keep the rocket on target.

Although we often speak of the computer as making decisions, in reality it is the programmer who decides, or rather, it is the programmer who determines the conditions under which the computer will execute one or another set of instructions. The computer does nothing on its own, but only what some programmer has told it to do. If the programmer gives incorrect instructions, the computer will blithely follow them. In this respect the computer is no more than an infinitely more complex cuckoo clock, which is only as accurate as the skill of the clockmaker. But where a faulty cuckoo clock might result only in a missed appointment, the consequences of a failure in a computer program can be drastic indeed.

The cuckoo clock affected the lives of those who depended on it although it provided only a single piece of information (the correct time), and even the earliest computers quickly became indispensable for solving all kinds of mathematical problems. But the ultimate difference between the computer and the cuckoo clock lies in the computer's generalized ability to process almost any kind of information, not just the value of a formula or the time of day. Stock transactions and bank transfers can be instantly ordered and credited. Telephones can be made to hold calls, to transfer or reject calls, to remember who called while the line was busy, all by prior instruction to a computer. Photographs and movies can be enhanced, colorized, and even completely altered through computer graphics. Pacemakers can adjust a heart's rhythm instantly in response to the changing state of the heart muscles. Our era has barely begun to explore the possibilities of the computer, and yet it is already known as the Computer Age.

But each new use of the computer's abilities means a new demand on the programmer's talents. The early days of simple computation of a mathematical formula have long since given way to complex manipulations of vast quantities of data, with each innovation giving rise to demands for more—and all of it is controlled by some programmer's instructions to a machine that is both blindingly fast and witheringly intolerant of error. This almost inhuman requirement for accuracy in computer programming has both philosophical and practical ramifications. The next chapters and Part IV explore some of these issues, while Parts II and III explain some of the means by which we ease the burden of dealing with them.

2

IS THERE AN AESTHETIC

OF PROGRAMMING?

A program is a set of detailed instructions given to a computer to perform a specific task. The computer will take no action without such instructions. In this respect, the computer is no different from a shovel. Just as a shovel will do nothing on its own, and performs its function only when someone picks it up and shoves it into the dirt, so a computer does nothing unless we give it orders. It matters not whether the motivating force is muscle power or typed commands; what is important is the motivation, which in all cases comes from the human mind.

It is therefore appropriate to speak of computer programming, as we speak of all other human activities, as having an aesthetic aspect. While aesthetics might be dismissed as merely expressing a concern for appearances, its encouragement of elegance does have practical advantages. Even so prosaic an activity as digging a ditch is improved by attention to aesthetics; a ditch dug in a straight line is both more appealing and more useful than one that zigzags at random, although both will deliver the water from one place to the other. Getting a computer program to deliver its intended result is a far more complex task than digging a ditch from a well, and attention to the aesthetic aspects ought to be an essential part of the process.

To begin with, there are aesthetic concerns inherent in the design of a program. Every program is the expression in computer language of a series of actions that the computer needs to take in order to solve a problem. Each such action or set of actions, when described in theoretical terms, is called an *algorithm*. While there may be a seemingly endless number of algorithms that can be used to solve a problem, some are more efficient, more elegant—more aesthetically correct—than others.

Consider, for example, the designing of a house. Did the architect put the bathroom near the bedrooms, or at the other end of the hall? And are there enough bathrooms for the people who will be living there? Is the kitchen near enough to the bathrooms to use the same water supply, or will extra money need to be spent to lay more pipes? Are there useless corners and dead ends? How much sunlight will each room have? There is not necessarily one right answer to any of these questions—it may be that putting the bathroom near the bedrooms justifies the cost of extra pipe—but it is clear that there are better designs and there are worse designs. The better designs are more aesthetically pleasing because they are more efficient and take more considerations into account.

The same is true with programming design. Although we use algorithms instead of blueprints, the same types of questions need to be raised: Is this piece of the structure necessary? Will it get in the way of other parts? Is it too far from—or too close to—

other steps in the process? How much weight should be given to each part in order to achieve an overall balance? Is there another, more efficient way to reach the same solution? And, of course, what can be done to ensure that this is a correct solution?

Suppose I want to look up a name in a telephone directory. I could start at the beginning of the book, and examine every name to see if it matches the one I am looking for. If I find it, then I can stop; otherwise I get to the end of the book and know that the name is not in there.

While it will work, such an algorithm — such a means of solving the problem — is hardly elegant or efficient. A much better approach to finding the name is to open the book near to where the first letter of the name is likely to be, then to go backwards or forwards in the book according to whether the name I want is before or after the name in the book that I am pointing to right now. I repeat this process until I either find the name, or else find two names next to each other, such that the name that I want would have been between them; in this case, the name is not in the book. This method yields its result — found or not found — much faster than the first one. It is much less taxing, and there is an aesthetic appeal to it with which the brute force method of the first technique cannot compete.

It is also readily understandable to a human being. Aesthetics, let us admit, mean nothing to a computer. And elegance in programming is by no means a guarantor of efficiency. It must be constantly borne in mind, however, that programs are not written solely to be understood by computers, but by people as well. While the computer may well be able to execute a poorly designed program and produce the correct answer, it is often difficult to determine from an examination of the program that it *is* the correct answer. Badly designed programs are notoriously error-prone, are likely to be slower, and are often referred to by derisive nicknames such as "spaghetti code"—for the logic paths resemble nothing so much as a bowl of spaghetti and are even harder to untangle. The very programmer who wrote such a piece of code might find it hard to trace its logic a week or a month later on. Moreover, even if the program does the proper job today, tomorrow may bring a new set of requirements. Programs constantly evolve, or to be more precise, the uses of a program evolve, and it is the programmer who performs the evolution. The requirements of modern programming assignments are such that they place an almost inhuman—and certainly inhumane—burden of perfection on fallible human beings, who will find an all-but-impossible job that much harder if the program's design is not perceptible to them. Attention to aesthetics improves human perception.

Another area of programming where aesthetics is involved is in the structure of the data. Take the previous example of the telephone book. The more efficient algorithm only worked because the data was organized alphabetically. A phone book in random order would indeed require the first, brute force algorithm of examining every entry, and a company that produced such a book would probably not last long. Most computer data structures are more complex than a phone book, and attention to the aesthetic aspects of their design will result both in more efficient processing of the data and faster understanding by the human programmers who must work with them.

The requirement for elegance involves not just the design of the algorithm and the internal data layout but the design of the input and output as well. The organization of information being entered, and the way the answers appear on the screen or the printed page, make a great deal of difference in their ability to be understood by the human beings who use them, although once again, it means nothing to the computer. Lives have been lost because a computer operator could not make sense of the data displayed.[†]

This aspect of aesthetics often goes by the name *ergonomics*. The science of ergonomics studies how people relate to the machines they use and tries to make such use more comfortable and more efficient. The design of the office chair is one obvious application of ergonomics. But it also applies to the computer programs that people use. A program, as I shall discuss later in detail, generally interacts with human beings at various points, particularly in accepting raw data as input and producing its results as finished output.

At every airline ticket counter there is a computer terminal. The airline agent, using a keyboard, fills in various fields on the screen—name of the passenger, destination, checked luggage, number of screaming children, and so on. The computer then checks its files to validate the reservation, makes a seat assignment if one was not already made, and prints out the boarding pass and baggage stickers. In processing all this, the computer—that is to say, the computer program, which is ultimately to say the computer programmer—must accept and display this information in such a way that the ticket agent can easily digest it and pass it on. Boarding passes, to take but one small part of the example, have (or should have) the seat number printed in large type in a blank area, which is easier for the passenger to see.

[†]The U.S.S. Vincennes shot down an Iranian civilian airplane in large part because the crewmen were confused by the way the data was presented on the computer screen. See Chapter 17 for more about this and other examples of how people died because of computer errrs.

In the early days of computing, aesthetics was a luxury programmers felt they could ill afford. Space and time were at a premium, computers were slow, and any trick that programmers could play with the design, any extra space they could squeeze out of the data, was a savings well earned. While computer costs have dropped dramatically, this short-cut mentality still endures. Moreover, computer programmers are just as susceptible as everyone else to failing to take the long view; all too often an algorithm, a technique, or a data layout that was meant to be a temporary quick-and-dirty fix becomes etched in stone — or at least in silicon.

A dramatic example of this insufficient attention to consequences is the potential for disaster presented by the year 2000 problem. Early computers, and the punched cards they used for input, were very short on space and often used a two-digit field to represent the year. Everyone understood that "50" meant "1950." But no one stopped to think that a computer program that interpreted "50" as "1950" would also interpret "00" as "1900" instead of 2000 — or if some did think about it, they thought that a program written in 1950 would be long gone by the turn of the century.

Many of these early programs and the computers they ran on are indeed relics of the past. But the algorithms and the data layouts that were developed for them still haunt us today; each succeeding incarnation of these programs was written to carry on the program of before, and the habits of an earlier generation propagated their way through new generations of programmers. Now we are faced with a horrendous effort to track down, upgrade, test, and install every single program — and there are millions — that relies on knowing what year it really is. The IRS, the Social Security Administration, even so simple an object as an elevator which is programmed to shut down if it has not had maintenance in the past six months, all are vulnerable because of our carelessness in restricting our representation of a year to a single century.

A greater concern for the long-term consequences of our casual programming decisions would have gone a long way toward minimizing the problems the year 2000 is causing us. While such a concern is not normally classified as an aesthetic principle, one of the qualities of elegance is its longevity — an acknowledgment that our constructions may well live longer than we first thought and should therefore be designed for the long term. There is also an aesthetic factor in recognizing that one's design may, even must, evolve to meet unanticipated challenges. Growth — for programs as well as for living things — can be orderly, well designed, elegant — or it can be ungainly and grotesque, a cancerous mass. The inexorability of time should have taught us in no uncertain terms that such growth *will* occur; our only choice is whether to guide it or to be consumed by it.

A working list of the aesthetic principles of programming might read as follows:

1) *The program has an elegant design.* Each step in the design follows logically from the previous one, and the flow from step to step is in the same direction. Each step performs one task.

2) *The program evolves.* A program that is written for one purpose will often be used to handle related but different situations, and the design must allow for expansion. The program must be flexible enough to grow, and to grow neatly.

3) *The program will last longer than you think.* It is often tempting to write an ungainly, sloppy "quick fix" to solve an urgent problem. But it often happens that the same program will be needed for other similar problems, or it is discovered that it can be used as the foundation for a larger program. Once this occurs, changing the original design of the program is effectively impossible. Better to start off right in the first place.†

4) *The program has a limited life span.* No matter how much thought is given to design, expansion, and new requirements, eventually a program will become so ungainly and so overburdened with tasks that it becomes error-prone and difficult to maintain. A programmer must be prepared to recognize this when it occurs and to write a new program rather than pile more complexities onto an old one.

5) *The data is well laid out.* The data is organized so that it can be quickly and accurately accessed for the purposes of the program, and so that it is readily understood by anyone who needs to write code to manipulate it. The data structure also allows for expansion.

6) *The program and data structures are explained.* Each algorithm, each step in the program, has comments and other documentation that describe what it does in clear and concise prose. Each part of the data layout includes a description of what it is used for. Any shortcuts or other tricks are thoroughly explained and well marked. This should be the

---

†*A classic example of this is Ward Christiansen's XMODEM protocol, which he wrote in a hurry one night because he needed a way to transfer some files between two PCs. Others heard about it and asked for a copy, and they in turn passed it on. Then it began to be used in commercial software, and even today XMODEM, for all its sloppiness and inefficiency, is one of the most popular file transfer protocols around.

most obvious principle of all. All too often it is not, and failure to observe it costs the industry untold hours of lost productivity.

All of the ideas I have discussed here are well known to many programmers; the current crop grew up with structured programming, well-defined data layouts, and in recent years have become familiar with object-oriented principles. True, it is rare for us to call them by the term "aesthetics." Yet I group them together under this heading because, as I said in the beginning, aesthetics is a profoundly human concept that speaks to peculiarly human needs. A programmer must always keep in mind that other human beings will use this code, will have to maintain, evolve, and ultimately replace this code, and will be profoundly affected in all aspects of life by what this code does or fails to do. Calling it aesthetics reminds us of the human dimension.

3

THE ETHICAL QUOTIENT

Ethics may be understood to mean a set of philosophical principles that govern our conduct, with the primary focus being on human interaction. Any object constructed or used by human beings in a way that affects other human beings therefore carries with it elements of ethical concern. While this applies to any of the tools we have created and used over the years, there are characteristics unique to computers and computer programming that present us with ethical challenges unlike any we have ever faced before. In brief, these include the qualities of magnification, precision, alienation, believability, malleability of information, impermeability, and autonomy of operation.

By *magnification* I mean the power of any tool to magnify our personal abilities. But unlike earlier tools, or even what we are accustomed these days to thinking of as tools, the computer magnifies our thoughts more than our muscles, and does so to a greater degree than any previous tool ever could. Whereas a book-keeper in a firm keeps track of as many customer accounts as can be humanly read and updated in a day, a programmer can direct a computer to monitor thousands or millions of accounts in that same period of time. A sailor might watch two, three, or four planes on a radar screen in an effort to determine if they are hostile or peaceful; a computer processing that same data might be able to track dozens of planes at once. The local cop on the beat may know the faces and habits of a few dozen local criminals; the computer back at the precinct house is collecting data about thousands of them all over the city. Government clerks plod slowly and sometimes inaccurately through income tax returns, while a computer can check a hundred taxpayers' calculations in a fraction of a second.

But magnification of thought in this way means that mistaken and malicious thoughts are also magnified. The computer possesses no moral compass, no more than any other tool; it cannot distinguish good from evil or truth from error unless we carefully instruct it to do so. An unscrupulous programmer could write a bookkeeping or banking program to transfer money from unsuspecting customers into a private account. Or an outside thief might discover an unanticipated contingency in the programming and use it as a license to steal. A program to help decide whether an approaching aircraft is hostile might have inadvertently left out a display of altitude changes—a crucial element in determining a plane's intentions. A database on criminals might not allow an operator to delete entries where the accused was found innocent, or might confuse two people who have similar names, or might not bother to distinguish between an arrest warrant for murder and a twenty-year-old parking violation. Outdated IRS computers, while still faster than a human clerk, are not fast enough to keep up with the flood of tax returns, nor are they always updated accurately to include changes in the tax code. The computer magnifies all our thoughts uncritically, both for good and for ill. It is we human beings who must choose which thoughts the computer follows and how it follows them.

The difficulty we face in doing so is partly explained by the next ethical conundrum the computer poses: the need for *precision*. Instructions to a computer must be precise in every detail, with no ambiguity, or the program will go off in some unintended direction or even fail completely just when it is needed most. Every contingency must be planned for in advance; the computer has no ability to make new decisions on its own, but can decide only in accordance with instructions we have already given it. There have been considerable advances in programming techniques designed to provide just this sort of precision and to make allowances for each possible situation. Yet completeness remains an unreachable goal as the increasingly complex demands we make on computers and their programs generate an exponential increase in the details associated with them. Any program of any size and consequence requires constant monitoring and maintenance.

In addition, the tendency of the computer to isolate programmers and operators from the people impacted by their actions fosters a new degree of *alienation*, which increases the problems created by its magnification of our imprecise thoughts. We are accustomed to making ethical decisions about how we use our tools according to the immediate and visible consequences of those decisions. But when we are separated from the people affected by our actions, this distance—this alienation— often provides us with an excuse to overlook the connection. This temptation long predates the computer, of course. A building contractor using inferior materials in the expectation of being long gone from the scene when the walls collapse is but one infamous example. The facility with which the computer alienates perpetrator from victim, however, adds a new dimension to an ancient concern. We no longer see a real person, only numbers and names on a computer screen. People who would never have the temerity to rob passers-by on the street have no compunctions about using a computer to steal their credit reputations instead—and do far more damage in the process. Negligence in keeping a database up-to-date or carelessness in data entry can have disastrous consequences for the person whose record has been mishandled. It has happened that a person is arrested again and again on the basis of the same mistaken information because the original error in the database was never corrected or the dismissal of the case was never entered. Such a cavalier attitude is credible because the database operator never deals with anything but streams of data that all seem the same, so the operator does not connect them with the real people they represented.

The phenomenon of alienation works on the programmer even more than on operators or users. Instead of seeing the program as a real instrument affecting the lives of real people, programmers sometimes see it as a game, a challenge to their ingenuity. The alienating quality of the computer permits us to overlook the human consequences of a programming decision or error. An assignment to link scattered databases in different computers, for example, becomes nothing more than a problem to be solved; the programmer does not notice the resulting diminution of privacy and the increased opportunities for mischief that can result.

That we can allow ourselves to be so blind to the consequences of the collection of personal information is a result of how the computer approaches this data. To the computer and its programs, data about a person is no different from data about the physical world. Both are quantities to be manipulated according to mathematical formulas. The alienating quality of the computer is such that it can reduce a living person to nothing more than numbers in a machine.

Alienation in the form of mediation—which is to say, the computer as mediator or intermediary—works on the user as well. People who would be unfailingly polite to strangers on the street do not hesitate to hurl insults at them on the Internet. The computer separates people from the person at the other end; they are not insulting a fellow human being, only a message on the screen. Again, this is a phenomenon with ancient roots, but one that is magnified by the ability of the computer to isolate us from those who are affected by our actions. The anonymity that the computer offers is not always as complete as it allows us to pretend—the computer may well keep records of our actions that we never know about until a much later confrontation—but the semblance, at least, of anonymous escape presents a great temptation for both deliberate and careless harm. It is ironic that the same Internet that allows us to interact with a wide variety of people that we might never otherwise meet also allows (and in some sense even encourages) behavior that alienates all who are not exactly of like mind.

Alienation and its concomitant anonymity figure in yet another aspect of the computer that raises ethical concerns, and that is its *believability*. The development of the computer and modern society have each been encouraged by each other in a kind of symbiosis; each growth spurt by one part stimulates a matching leap by the other part. As a result, our society and its institutions have become so large and so complex that without computers they would instantly dissolve. Imagine for a moment trying to run the Social Security system, or a modern bank, or even a warehouse, without computers. But this same dependence has resulted in a necessity to believe what the computer tells us: whether the Social Security recipient is alive or dead, or how much money is in a customer's account, or whether we have sufficient stock on hand to fill an order. Because the computer has allowed us to collect and maintain far more information than we could before, it has also made us almost totally dependent on it to produce valid information. The computer simply provides us with too much information too fast for us to do anything more than assume it is correct.

This assumption of correctness has been further strengthened by our acute awareness of the computer's arithmetic abilities. We can easily verify the results when a computer calculates 2 plus 2. But when we ask it to multiply 9,785.63 by 10,348.27, we are not inclined to question it when it reports the answer as 101,264,341.3601. We expect the computer to compute, in the original meaning of the word: to perform arithmetic calculations, and to do them flawlessly.[†]

But now we have transferred this aura of infallibility from calculation to information, although there is no guarantee of its correctness beyond that of the skill of the operator who entered the data and the programmer who wrote the instructions to manipulate it. If the National Crime Information Center computer

[†]This assumption is not always warranted. After Intel Corporation introduced its new Pentium processor in 1994, mathematicians discovered that when it divided certain specific numbers, it was off by .006%, or approximately 61 parts per million. In some cases, this meant that the fourth or fifth significant digit was incorrect. Intel released a corrected chip in December 1994 (Moler [1994]).

reports an outstanding warrant, the police are far more likely to believe it than the protests of the hapless victim who claims they are arresting an innocent man. Unexpunged parking violation tickets, theft and assumption of another's identity, carelessness in cleaning up case backlogs—all have resulted in citizens who were going about their lawful business being detained and forced to prove their innocence against the word of the computer.[†] We have gone beyond dependence on the computer to an expectation or assumption of its omniscience that is seductive but unwarranted and very dangerous to us both individually and as a society.

Even if the data were correctly entered and properly manipulated and displayed, there remains the danger that it can be changed without our being aware of it. The data storage media of a computer—the disks and tapes—are designed to be *malleable*, that is, they can write new information in the same place where old data was stored, wiping out all traces of its previous contents. Unlike a mark in a book which, even if in pencil, leaves behind a hint that it has been erased and changed, marks in a computer are magnetic signals whose change of polarity must be free of taint. There are some devices on the market, such as CD-ROMs, which can be written on only once; after that, they can only be read (although there is also a growing market for rewritable CDs). Programming techniques that guarantee the integrity of data, and record any changes made to an existing record, are in somewhat wider use, particularly among financial institutions. But if the programmer does not conscientiously apply these techniques, our assumption of data integrity becomes little more than an exercise in credulity.

This is but one example of how the characteristic of believa-

[†]See Forester and Morrison (1994, 131–37), for a sampling of actual cases.

bility extends beyond the data in a computer to the programs that manipulate it. Our trust in the integrity of the program is a consequence of our inability to examine the workings of the computer for ourselves. Even into the middle years of the twentieth century, we could peer inside our machines and persuade ourselves that we understood what they were doing. It takes relatively little mechanical aptitude to understand the general principles behind the internal combustion engine, the tool that most transformed the world between 1900 and 1950. But the machine that has had an even greater impact on the latter half of the century is *impermeable* to casual observation. If a spark plug fails in a car, an ordinary person with little training could replace it, or if not, would quickly understand a mechanic's explanation of the problem. An examination of even so simple a computer as that which sits inside a watch, however, provides little in the way of comprehension. The circuits in a microchip cannot even be separately distinguished by the naked eye, and generally mean nothing to anyone except an expert trained in their design.

And when it comes to the programs that actually make the computer work, the degree of this impermeability becomes effectively absolute. Software—a computer program—is not, as a rule, available in a form which can be comprehended by a human being; programs are sold in packages that can be understood only by the computer circuits directly. There are obvious commercial reasons for this: Programmers who have spent years developing code are not likely to want to distribute it in a way that lets someone else build on it and thereby reap unearned benefits. Source code—a program in a form that a person can read—is also useless unless converted into the binary language of the machine, and the average computer user is not likely to have the skills or tools needed for this often complex task. Finally, even if the general user were to see the original source, it would most likely be meaningless; only someone who is expert in the specific computer language has a hope of understanding just what it is that a program of any size is doing.

The user is consequently forced to rely on the programmer's or salesperson's assurance that the program will do what it is advertised to do. The difficulty of guaranteeing software performance can be glimpsed from the discussion above, and will be further explored in later chapters. From an ethical perspective, however, the impermeability of software presents a further complication: It makes it almost impossible to know if the software was deliberately designed to act to the disadvantage of the user for the benefit of the programmer or supplier.

There are, for example, Internet service providers that will conduct a search of systems around the world on the user's behalf, looking for information as arcane as graduate papers on the style of clothing worn by English peasants in the fifteenth century. Unbeknownst to the user, some of these "search engines" will implant a data structure in the user's computer, which the service provider will use to accumulate information about the user's interests and search patterns.† The intention of the programmer may have been to aid the user in subsequent searches by recording search habits and favored sites with the aim of becoming a more efficient helper. But the result is that the program now has access to private information about the user, and the user has no control over its use and distribution. If I go to a library and sit down to read a book on the stock market, there is no chance that a week later I will receive a letter from some stockbroker soliciting my business. The act of looking up stock prices on the

---

†For obscure reasons, such a structure is often called a "cookie."

Internet, however, could very well result in just such an e-mail invitation. Information about our interests and habits is being collected and sold without our consent (or even awareness) because there is no way for ordinary users to look into the programs on their computers—much less the remote computers they are connected to—and see what they are really doing.[†]

An even more pernicious application of this quality of impermeability is the computer virus. This is a program that is hidden inside another program and causes some undesired action to occur. The virus may be as innocuous as a message flashed on the computer screen at random or as serious as the total destruction of accumulated data. In addition, it has the capacity to replicate itself and spread to other computers, doing more damage as it goes. A whole industry has developed in the last few years to provide antivirus programs that constantly scan the computer and any new program that is loaded into it, looking for evidence of viruses; they also monitor disk accesses for signs of viral activity. But this has led to an equal effort on the part of the virus programmers to defeat these guards; it has become a game to them, and the alienating quality of the computer shields them from the consequences of their mischief.

That one human being can do such damage to another from such a distance in this way is a demonstration of yet another characteristic of the computer: *autonomy of operation*. To a greater extent than any other tool we have created, the computer is capable of acting without our intervention or supervision. Sim-

[†]Newer versions of Internet search engines—browsers—have closed some of the loopholes that enabled remote sites to read and record a user's address, and developers are constantly working on ways to improve "cookie" security. And of course most Internet sites are honorable. But there are always those who seek to exploit any weakness in the Internet in order to collect and sell information that was not intended to be given to them.

ple computers such as those in watches or microwaves can operate in no other way; there are simply no controls or means of reprogramming them to modify their ways of doing things once they leave the factory. And the speed with which larger, more complex computers operate makes it impractical for human beings to monitor their every move. But this very autonomy makes them vulnerable to the kind of attack for which a virus was designed. Since it is impossible for us to monitor the computer's every action, we may miss the undesired actions of a virus or other insidious program until it is too late.[†]

From a programmer's perspective, the ethical implication of this autonomy of operation is that it demands a meticulous attention to detail. The programmer is preparing a series of instructions to be given to a computer to execute while the programmer is no longer there. And the computer has no leeway or latitude in carrying out its orders except those the programmer has given it; thus each instruction must be precise and clear, and in some way deal with all the possibilities that the program can confront. The programmer's responsibility is far more consuming than that of an officer giving a command to a troop of soldiers, who are expected to use judgment and good sense in carrying out their orders. The computer has neither.

In the early days of computing, this quality of autonomy gave rise to great expectations of robots trained to do our bidding, subways and trains operating at high speeds with no human engineer, giant factories totally remote-controlled. In practice, true autonomy has proven to be an elusive goal, largely because of

---

[†]For reasons to be explored later, personal computers are most susceptible to viruses. Larger computers have much greater protections against malicious or inadvertent damage, and dedicated microchips in appliances cannot be corrupted once they have left the factory.

the enormous difficulty in accounting for all the contingencies that may occur. A program of any complexity that runs in the real world is eventually going to be faced with some situation that the programmer did not anticipate and that the code therefore will not deal with correctly. Software companies maintain large service staffs to deal with just such customer problems. Data centers are constantly manned by operators watching over the computers, and in many cases programmers are expected to be available by pager, much as doctors are, to deal with the computer equivalent of a cerebral hemorrhage.

Yet the expectation of autonomy persists, and there is just enough reality to this perception that we as a society have become dependent on flawless and continuous service from our electronic servants. When they fail we find ourselves unnerved; the dreaded phrase "the computer is down" has become a tocsin for inaction and feelings of helpless rage. But the computer did not fail. The programmers, the designers, the operators, the users — they failed. The claim that "the computer screwed up" is as facile and as worthless an excuse as that hoary attempt at exculpation "the devil made me do it." Autonomy of operation is a reminder of our responsibilities; it is not a shield to hide behind.[†]

All technology confronts us with an ethical question: Even though our tools are capable of certain actions, does it necessarily follow that we ought to use them that way? Just because we can

[†]The Association for Computing Machinery (ACM) has compiled a code of ethics and professional conduct that it recommends to its members. Among its primary imperatives are that programmers must be aware of the potential for harm and do their best to avoid it (§ 1.2), and to "maintain the privacy and integrity of data describing individuals" (§ 1.7). The code, however, contains no provision for enforcement beyond termination of membership in the ACM (§ 4.2) (Communications of the ACM 36, no. 2 [February 1993]: 96–105).

does not mean we should. Any ethical structure recognizes that human beings are capable of doing deeds that are ethically incorrect and that it therefore forbids; we are slow, however, in coming to the realization that these codes of ethics must be extended to apply to our autonomous tools as well.

Many of our ideas of ethical behavior derive from our ancestral patterns of living in villages and small agrarian communities where everyone knew everyone else, and trust (or the lack thereof) was a product of close and continuing personal interaction. The city has always posed a problem for ethicists because, while it creates a concentration of people and thus facilitates the exchange and development of ideas, goods, and capital, it also provides anonymity for the thief and the guttersnipe. It makes an easy hiding place where the evil, the incompetent, and the merely careless can escape facing responsibility for their actions. The computer, particularly in its manifestation on the Internet, has often been likened to a global village. But a more accurate analogy would be a global city, presenting all the problems as well the potentials that a human city holds.

Part II

THE

STRUCTURE

OF

THE

COMPUTER

4

TYPES OF COMPUTERS

Real programs are written to run on real computers, so before discussing the techniques of programming it is necessary to examine the machines that the programs will run on. While the history of the computer as a viable tool spans less than fifty years, in that time many different types of computers have appeared on the scene, and the terms used to describe them have had as much to do with the time of their appearance as with the true nature of these machines. A brief review of the history of computers is therefore in order.[†]

World War II was responsible for a great many sudden changes in the world, from the birth of atomic energy to the death of

[†]For a thorough analysis of the history of the computer and its predecessors, see Campbell-Kelly and Aspray (1996). Kidwell and Ceruzzi (1994) is also a good general history, while Ritchie (1986) and Slater (1987) concentrate on the personalities of the early pioneers. Some other general histories are included in the bibliography.

colonialism. It was also the impetus for exponential growth in science and industry; the war demanded extraordinary efforts in improving mass production, in building new fighter planes, in monitoring troop movements, and in deciphering enemy codes. Both the American and British governments invested great sums of money and talent in new calculating machines needed to help in battle, creating among other things decryptors to crack German ciphers, differential calculators to produce artillery firing tables and to figure the implosion requirements for the atomic bomb, and simulators to train fighter pilots. It is ironic that the war ended before most of these machines were anywhere near completion; only the Colossus (developed by the British to outwit the German Enigma cipher machine) and the Harvard Mark I were fully productive.

With the end of the war, the participants in the EDVAC, ENIAC, and similar projects began to think about the commercial possibilities of this new electronic stored-program calculating machine. Presper Eckert and John Mauchly, veterans of the ENIAC and EDVAC projects, founded their own company in Philadelphia in 1946 and persuaded the Census Bureau to buy a computer that they proposed to develop and build for a price of $300,000. Unfortunately, they were better at engineering than at economics, and when it became clear that the new computer would cost over a million dollars to manufacture, they were forced to turn to outside investors, and ultimately sold the company to Remington Rand, though they remained on the project as employees.[†] The revived product, called the UNIVAC I, was

---

[†]Eckert and Mauchly also ran afoul of the red-baiting hysteria of the times; Mauchly recalls being asked once if he was aware that a former college roommate of a company employee was a "card-carrying Communist." Either this connection or some

finally delivered to the Census Bureau in 1951. It was the first commercial American computer, and for several years the name UNIVAC was synonymous with computers in the public mind.

All computers operate by switching an electronic signal on or off in response to some other electronic signal. The first device to do this was the relay, an electro-mechanical device that was in either a closed, completed state (on), or else in an open, incomplete state (off), depending on whether or not a current was passing through its magnet. Relays, of course, are slow, their reaction times measured in tenths of a second. A vacuum tube can perform the same function as a relay with no mechanical movement whatsoever and is therefore much faster than a relay. Vacuum tubes, however, must be heated in order to operate, and they have a relatively short lifespan. Presper Eckert extended the life of the ENIAC's 18,000 tubes by never turning off the heaters (Campbell-Kelly and Aspray 1996, 88).

In late 1947, inventors at AT&T's Bell Labs produced the first successful transistor. The transistor behaved like a vacuum tube or a relay, but it used wires embedded in a solid, semiconducting material instead of filaments in a vacuum. It was faster, cheaper, far more reliable, and generated much less heat in the process.[†] By the late 1950s the transistor was well on the way to replacing the vacuum tube as the driving mechanism of the computer. IBM's 1401 computer, an all-transistor model introduced in 1959, became the most widely marketed computer of the time. (Much of its success was also due to its new high-speed printer.)

---

other equally innocuous association cost the company a chance for a Navy contract (Stern 1981, 114).
[†]The 5,000 tubes of the UNIVAC I put out so much heat that engineers working on it in Philadelphia routinely stripped to shorts and undershirts during the summer (Campbell-Kelly and Aspray 1996, 121).

The 1401 was designed for business and accounting applications. At around the same time, IBM also introduced its 7090 series, which was oriented toward processing scientific calculations. Neither machine had compatible parts, nor could programs written for one machine work on the other. Similar incompatibilities plagued the rest of IBM's product line and were in fact an industry-wide problem. In 1964, IBM released an all-new series of computers—the System/360—that were compatible with each other and could do both business and scientific calculations: true general-purpose computers. Most of IBM's competitors either followed suit or left the field entirely.

All of these machines were large and often were referred to by the term "mainframe," a reference to the main housing that held the central components. They were also expensive to purchase, rent, and operate; thus they were most likely to be used by large corporations and universities that could afford the capital outlay and maintenance overhead, while smaller firms and colleges would rent time from a computer vendor. New manufacturers who could not compete with IBM for the mainframe market saw a niche here waiting to be filled by smaller, cheaper machines. Digital Equipment Corporation (DEC) is credited with introducing the first successful minicomputers, the PDP-5 in 1963 and the PDP-8 in 1965.[†]

Minicomputers were feasible because of a new advance in electronics: the integrated circuit. Previously, transistors had been mounted on a circuit board laced with wires. An integrated circuit etched both the transistors and their connections onto a sin-

---

[†]See Kidwell and Ceruzzi (1994, 77). The term "minicomputer" seems to have been coined by John Leng of DEC's branch office in the United Kingdom. He may have been inspired by the miniskirt just then arriving on the London fashion scene, or perhaps by the Morris Mini Motor car (ibid.).

gle compact surface. As with the transistor over the vacuum tube, the integrated circuit (or "chip") provided faster and more reliable service at a cheaper cost and with less heat. Because of the reduced heat factor, it was possible to package more chips closer together, further reducing the distance between components, thus increasing the speed of operation and also augmenting the processing power of the minicomputer. Invented in 1962, the first integrated circuit contained perhaps a half-dozen components; by 1996 chips that held as many as fifteen million transistors were being manufactured.[†]

Integrated circuits soon found their way into mainframes as well, but by then the minicomputer market had been firmly established. Today the difference between mainframes and minicomputers is partly a matter of which computer they are descended from: an IBM-style, large-scale, massive "number-cruncher" of the 1960s or a DEC-type, smaller-but-cheaper box of the 1970s. Mainframes are also more capable of handling large volumes of data, but in terms of speed and functionality there is often little to distinguish the two.

Yet both mainframes and minicomputers were still expensive enough to be out of reach for the individual user, who was still dependent on an office, school, or vendor for computer access. It was the further development of integrated circuit technology that was responsible for yet another innovation whose impact is immense and still ongoing. As etching technology became more refined, it became possible to put more and more transistors on a single board and make that board smaller and smaller, until finally it became possible to fit an entire central processing unit

[†]For a discussion of the history and types of integrated circuits and how they are manufactured, see Freedman (1991: 124–31).

onto a single silicon wafer: a microprocessor. The first such chips began to appear around 1971, and in 1974 Intel Corporation introduced the 8080, one of the first commercially successful microprocessors. This chip, complete with its housing and connections, was a little over two inches long, about a half-inch wide and just over a quarter-inch thick; it contained the equivalent of 5,000 transistors and could run a computer program in much the same way as a mini or mainframe.

It is perhaps impossible to overstate the impact of the microprocessor. Its reduction in price and increase in computing power have, in less than twenty years, totally transformed our world. It is at the heart of the *embedded system* — specialized hardware and software dedicated to a particular task. A computer faster and more sophisticated than a million-dollar UNIVAC I or a ten-thousand-dollar PDP-8 controls a five-dollar digital watch. A hearing aid small enough to fit inside the human ear contains a microprocessor that permits close to normal hearing. Microprocessors run microwaves and refrigerators, regulate automobile fuel lines to reduce pollution and increase gas mileage, record and transmit credit card purchases, answer telephones, set the pace of heartbeats, inject drugs, and make coffee in the morning. We have only just begun to explore uses for this tool.

But the greatest impact the microprocessor has had so far is that it made the development of the personal computer possible. Hobbyists were among the first to recognize the potential of the microprocessor to provide them with their own at-home computer on a desktop, but for several years in the late 1970s, the personal computer was little more than these hobbyists' expensive toy. Then, between 1978 and 1980, commercial manufacturers of both hardware and software began to realize its market potential, and by 1980 Apple Computer had produced the Apple II, a combination package of hardware and easily accessible software, and sold over 130,000 units. Business applications, games, and word processors had also made their first appearances by 1979. As far back as 1975, IBM had tried selling a desktop computer, and in 1980 it teamed up with Microsoft to develop an operating system (MS-DOS) for the new IBM PC, which it introduced in August, 1981. By 1983, the IBM PC had become the industry standard for personal computing — to the point that its product name, the "PC," is now the standard term for all computers of this type. The years since have seen an exponential growth of products, services, and hardware for the personal computer. The result has been that for the first time, the power of the computer has been placed directly into the hands of Everyman.

The computer, once the province of what might almost be called a secular priesthood, has now become a commonplace household appliance. Government and corporate mainframes with their vast databases still have an impact on our lives, but the personal computers on our desks are the ones we relate to. We use them to balance our checkbooks, write our letters, teach our children, play games with us. Small companies using business software on a PC can have the equivalent of a large corporation's accounting department at their disposal. Through the Internet, the personal computer is creating a worldwide electronic community; before the PC, selected universities, government agencies, and a few corporations could connect to the ARPAnet (the Internet's predecessor), but now even individual users can afford the necessary computing power.

Yet the PC's origins as a hobbyist's curiosity are reflected in the ungainly and cumbersome programs that, for many years, were all that could be run on them. MS-DOS, for example, the classic operating system for the IBM PC, used an arcane collection of shorthand commands that sometimes made sense to a computer science graduate but hopelessly confused the average consumer. The potential for a huge market also encouraged people with vastly varied programming skills to come up with software that looked to fill a need but was written with no understanding of programming conventions or user interactions. Such software all too often came with confusing, patronizing, or overly technical instructions, was released with minimum testing, and was sold with disclaimers explicitly renouncing any guarantee that the program would work as advertised — or would even work at all.[†]

The personal computer has the potential to provide tremendous power to the individual user. But that power is actually available only to the extent that some program has been written to take advantage of it. Since very few users have the years of training it takes to write their own programs, they are as much limited as empowered by the available programs for the PC. Nor does it necessarily do much good to complain; a diverse, diffuse collection of individual PC users rarely wields the clout of a large corporation that, with its purchasing power and in-house staff, can arrange for programs to be fixed, improved, tailored to its needs.

Although operating systems and applications for the personal

[†]The following statement attached to a 1996 financial planning program is typical of many such disclaimers: "We do not warrant, guarantee or make any representations regarding the use of, or the results of the use of, the Program in terms of correctness, accuracy, reliability, currentness or otherwise. You rely on the Program and its results solely at your own risk. . . . You will not hold [the vendor] or any other person who has been involved in the creation, production or delivery of the Program liable for any defect of, or error or omission in, the Program or documentation." The vendor did, however, warrant that the diskettes the program came on would be "free from defects in materials and workmanship under normal use and service for a period of 90 days from the date you receive it."

computer are improving, abstruse commands, peculiar data structures, obscure facilities, and unexpected obstacles are still rampant in the software commonly used on many PCs. And people still write completely idiosyncratic programs for the PC with the thought that there is some market out there willing to buy. What first attracted hobbyists to the PC, its almost anarchic expression of individuality, continues to be part of its drawing power. The personal computer offers to any individual willing to master it both the opportunities and the pitfalls that are the hallmarks of the creative power of programming.

5

THE PARTS OF A COMPUTER

All computers, whether mainframes, minicomputers, or personal computers, and even to some extent specialized microprocessors, share some parts in common. They all have a central processing unit that executes instructions, memory that holds these instructions and the data they operate on, and means of communicating with the outside world in order to receive data and transmit the results of their data manipulation.

It is this last part—the connection to the outside world—that confronts the average user, and when people speak of using the computer, it is this part that they generally mean. In the early years of computing, when machinery was expensive and access to it was strictly regimented, the average user never saw or touched a physical machine. Punched cards for input and paper printout for output were the norm. Nowadays we are able to provide each individual with direct access to the computer, and the user's terminal—whether connected to a simple PC or part of a vast network of such devices all using a mainframe computer somewhere far away—is the first thing that comes to mind when we think of the computer and our interaction with it.

From the perspective of the programmer, the terminal is actually two separate devices, even if they are physically combined: the *keyboard*, on which the user types commands and data to be sent to the computer as *input*, and the *monitor* (also called a screen, or sometimes a cathode-ray tube or CRT), through which the computer displays the results of its computations to the user as *output*. Because these are two separate devices, the characters the user types in on the keyboard do not automatically show up on the monitor; a computer program has to put them there.[†]

But even though the keyboard and the monitor are the parts of the computer we are most likely to see, they are nothing more than devices by which we communicate with the real computer, which is someplace else. The heart of the computer is the central processing unit, or CPU. Here are all the circuits that locate the next instruction to be executed, and the circuits that perform the steps needed to carry out that instruction. Here are the accumulators that hold the results of arithmetic calculations; here are the control registers, the index registers, and so on. This is the unit that actually performs the work dictated by the computer program.

For purposes of understanding how to program a computer, it is not necessary to go into details of how this circuitry functions, how the AND, OR, and NOT gates work, or what a pipeline is,

---

[†]The process of displaying typed input on the monitor is called "echoing." Not all typed input is echoed; in particular, we do not want to echo such things as passwords. When a user types in a password, what appears on the monitor is most often a series of X's or asterisks, or sometimes nothing at all.

no more than it is necessary to understand nerve-muscle coordination in order to raise one's arm. However, it is important to grasp the concept of how the actual instructions operate, even if, as we shall see in Part III, modern programmers rarely use these instructions directly.

All computers, from the smallest microchip in a household appliance to the largest mainframe in a bank's back office, operate by means of electronic circuits, which indicate the presence or absence of a current. Such a circuit can be constructed from a relay switch, vacuum tube, transistor, or an integrated circuit path, but they all have two possible states: present or absent, ON or OFF, one or zero, positive or negative. We represent this set of states by using the binary number system, which consists of two digits: zero and one. These binary circuits, each called a *bit*, are then grouped together to form larger numbers. For example, if four circuits grouped together have the states 1, 1, 0, and 1, respectively, then this group of four circuits holds the equivalent of the decimal number 13. The CPU is capable of dealing with a wide variety of bit groupings, up to 128 or more bits at a time, and the next chapter will go into these groupings in some detail. All that needs to be borne in mind for the moment is that the CPU operates on these groups of bits to produce its results.

Some of these groups will be data, while others will be instructions to perform operations on that data. Both instructions and data are contained in the next major part of the computer: the memory. Memory is temporary storage; that is, each element of memory is at any given instant set either to zero or one, and it holds that state only until the CPU executes an instruction to change it. Early memory units included such devices as a mercury delay line, which preserved its binary value by using acoustics, and the Williams tube, where an electron beam set or read the polarity of a phosphor on the tube face. Until the phosphor faded, the tube would "remember" the correct value.[†] These were soon replaced by magnetic memory units and later by chips which would retain their settings as long as power was supplied to them. In most cases, when the power is turned off the contents of memory disappear, but there are special situations where permanent memory is useful. This is called *read-only memory* (ROM), in which the numbers are part of the circuitry and cannot be changed. A variation on ROM is PROM—*programmable read-only memory*. As with ROM, the contents of the PROM do not disappear even when the power is turned off, but they can be changed by using a special machine or special machine instructions. (Because memory organization and contents are crucial to the understanding of programming, they will be covered in more detail in the next chapter.)

While the CPU gets its instructions and data from the main memory, this memory is limited in size; moreover, its contents are volatile and designed to be so, constantly changing as the CPU carries out its instructions. With the exception of specialized microprocessors (which generally use ROM or PROM to store their instructions), all types of computers use some sort of secondary storage to hold those programs and data that are not currently being used. The most common form of such storage is a *disk*, although tapes have also long been used, and CD-ROMs are now standard equipment on new PCs. (Disk structures are both versatile and complex, and they too deserve a chapter of their own.)

Disks, like the keyboards and monitors discussed earlier, are

[†]At the press conference to unveil the Williams tube, the device performed miserably; the flash bulbs from the press photographers' cameras were wiping out the data.

examples of *input/output devices,* more commonly called *I/O devices,* which are the link between the CPU and the outside world. Every computer must include some sort of I/O device through which it receives data and commands, reports its results, and otherwise performs its functions. A specialized microprocessor in a microwave, for example, has wires connecting it to the keypad and control buttons of the front panel, enabling it to receive the cook's commands to generate a specified amount of radiation for a set length of time. It has other wires connecting it to the microwave tube and to the turntable, and yet another to the bell that signals the cook when the job is done. A general-purpose computer will use general-purpose communications devices such as disks, floppy disks, keyboards, and monitors, as well as printers, modems, and specialized devices designed to meet a specific need. A PC will most likely have at most one of each, although

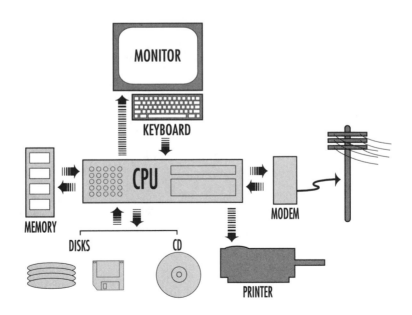

some now have the capacity to handle more. A minicomputer may connect to several hundred terminals, while a mainframe, such as one that runs an airline reservations system, may operate banks of disk drives while communicating with thousands of specially designed terminals around the world.

A *modem* is an I/O device that converts binary data into electronic signals that can be transmitted across a telephone line. At the other end of the phone connection is another modem, receiving these signals and converting them back to binary so that they can be understood by the recipient computer. Modems are used to connect two computers at a distance or to connect a remote terminal to a computer. One increasingly common use of modems is to connect a PC to a larger computer that is itself connected, by means of other modems, to the Internet.

Similarly, a *printer* is an output-only device that converts binary data into characters on a printed page. Early printers were capable of printing only a limited and fixed set of alphanumeric characters, but modern printers contain microchips that can create any number of character fonts as well as special characters, graphics, drawings, and color combinations, all governed by the binary signals sent down from memory by the CPU.

Input and output, then, are defined from the perspective of memory. Input goes into memory, and output comes out from it. It is thus to memory that we should now turn our attention.

6

THE CONSTRUCTION OF MEMORY

Memory is the stage on which the CPU performs. It contains the instructions of the program that the computer is currently executing, and it contains the data that this program is currently working on. Everything that resides on disk, that is entered on a keyboard, that is sent via modem, must somehow make its way to the memory in order to be used.

As was described in the previous chapter, all memory consists of circuits that are either on or off, positive or negative, one or zero. By combining these circuits into groups, we can represent numbers of various sizes, numbers that have meaning to the circuits of the CPU.

Each individual circuit of memory is called a *bit*, and the smallest usable grouping of bits is known as a *byte*. Over the years, several sizes of bytes have been tried, and the industry long ago settled on a grouping of eight bits as the most efficient byte size.

A byte of eight bits can hold 256 possible values (for reasons to be explained later), and thus can be used for the most common sorts of small numbers. Each byte is assigned an *address* in the memory boards; this address is a number that describes the physical location of the byte for the computer circuitry. The contents of the byte may be changed by any computer instruction; the address of the byte cannot.

The contents of this byte can take several forms. An obvious one is as a number in the range 0 through 255. When used this way, the byte can be a counter, an index into a list or array, and so on as the programmer finds a need. This is called an *unsigned byte*, since all the values it can hold are positive (with the exception of zero).

If the programmer needs to use a number that may be either positive or negative, then we need a *signed byte*, where one bit is set aside to represent the sign (positive or negative), and the remaining seven bits contain the number value. By convention, we use the first bit of eight for the sign; if it is zero, the byte is positive (zero is a positive number in this setup), while if it is one, then the byte contains a negative number. When a byte is used as a signed byte, it contains numbers in the range −128 through +127.

One of the most common ways to use a byte is as a character, the sort that is typed in from a keyboard and sent to a screen or printer. Let us establish a rule that the decimal value 65 will designate the uppercase letter "A," that 66 is used for "B," up to 90 for "Z." We will also designate the decimal values 97 through 122 as the lowercase letters "a" through "z." The numerals "0" through "9" will be represented by the numbers 48 through 57, while 36 is used for the dollar sign ($), 63 will be a question mark (?), and so on. Since a byte can hold any one of

256 possible values, there is plenty of room for all the standard characters found on a keyboard.

The numbers that I have just assigned to the various characters are in fact part of an actual industry standard known as ASCII (often pronounced "ASK-ee"), which stands for American Standard Code for Information Interchange. ASCII is used on most PCs and minicomputers as well as some mainframes. The other major standard currently in use is EBCDIC (pronounced "EBB-suh-dik"), or Electronic Binary-Coded Decimal Interchange Code. EBCDIC was developed by IBM for use on its System/360 series of computers, and is still used on IBM mainframes today.[†]

While the numerical values for these characters may appear arbitrary, in many cases they are not. For example, the numeric characters are defined consecutively starting with the number 48 for "0." Thus, to convert a numeric character into a signed or unsigned byte value so that we may calculate arithmetic with it, we subtract 48 from the ASCII value: decimal 49 (ASCII "1") minus 48 becomes the number 1. This conversion step is absolutely necessary; the user who types in the character "1" means to say the number 1, not the number 49. A similar conversion — adding 48 to the number 1 — is necessary in order to send the character representation of the number to a screen or printer. Sending the number 1 to the screen is *not* the same as sending the number 49; only the latter number will cause the character "1" to be displayed.

Another arithmetic operation that can be performed on a character is to convert uppercase letters to lowercase or vice versa. Each uppercase letter in ASCII standard is represented by a num-

[†]The Appendix contains a complete description of the standard ASCII codes.

ber that is exactly 32 less than its lowercase counterpart: "A" is 65, while "a" is 97. To change "A" to "a," add 32; to change "a" to "A," subtract 32. Using this technique, a programmer can write a program that accepts commands from the user without regard to the case in which they are entered. Thus, "COPY," "CoPy," and "copy" will all perform the COPY function; the command interpreter first converts all lowercase letters to uppercase and then looks up "COPY" in its list of commands.

While it may have been easier to follow this explanation by showing the decimal values of the various examples, within the byte itself all values are nothing more than a series of positive or negative currents preserved by the state of a relay, vacuum tube, transistor, magnetic core, or integrated circuit. The contents of a byte are really best described by using the binary number system, where the digits are ones and zeros, each digit representing the state of a bit in memory.

In the decimal number system, a number is a set of digits in the range zero through nine, and the value of the number is the sum of all its digits according to their position. For example, take the number 13. It has digits in two positions: a "3" in the ones (rightmost) position and a "1" in the tens position to the left of it. The value of this number is:

$$
\begin{array}{rcl}
3 \cdot 1 &=& 3 \\
+\ 1 \cdot 10 &=& 10 \\
\hline
&=& 13
\end{array}
$$

Each of the multipliers in the example above is an exact power of 10: $1 = 10^0$ and $10 = 10^1$. The exponent values (0 and 1, respectively) are the number of places from the rightmost digit of the number. The further away from the end of the number,

the greater the exponent, and the higher the value of its multi-
plier. Thus, since 3 is zero places away from the end, its multi-
plier is ten to the zeroth power, which is 1.

In the binary number system, the same principle applies, except that instead of each position being a power of ten, it is a
power of two. The binary number 1101, then, has its decimal
equivalent calculated this way:

$$
\begin{aligned}
1 \cdot 1 \ (2^0) &= \ 1 \\
+ \ 0 \cdot 2 \ (2^1) &= \ 0 \\
+ \ 1 \cdot 4 \ (2^2) &= \ 4 \\
+ \ 1 \cdot 8 \ (2^3) &= \ 8 \\
\hline
&= 13
\end{aligned}
$$

In this example I have included the powers of two, so that it
is easier to see that the exponent used in each multiplication (0,
1, 2, 3) matches the position of the digit in the number 1101.

A decimal number which consists of two positions (ones and
tens) can have a value in the range 00 through 99. A byte which
consists of eight such positions — that is, eight bits, each of which
has a value of zero or one — can hold binary values in the range
00000000 through 11111111. The decimal equivalent of these
binary numbers are, respectively, 0 and 255, which explains my
earlier statement that a byte can hold 256 possible values.[†]

To realize the value of describing a byte's contents in binary,
look again at the first two alphabetic letters of the ASCII character set:

[†]It is very important to bear in mind this distinction between the number of values
a byte can hold, and the highest value it can hold. To the computer, zero is *not* the
absence of a number; it is a number like any other and must be counted as one of
the possible values that a byte can hold. Many beginning programmers (and even
some experienced ones) have tripped over this subtle point.

CHARACTER	DECIMAL VALUE	BINARY VALUE
A	65	01000001
a	97	01100001

and

B	66	01000010
b	98	01100010

Each lowercase letter starts with the same value used for an uppercase letter, and then adds a one bit in the sixth position from the end: binary 00100000, which happens to be the decimal number 32 that was used earlier to convert uppercase letters to lowercase. With this understanding of the binary values of the ASCII set, all a programmer really has do in order to convert a string of alphabetics into uppercase is to turn off (change from 1 to 0) the sixth bit of each byte. It does not matter whether the bit was previously on or off; by forcing it to be off we ensure that the entire string is all in uppercase.

Binary representation also makes it clearer why the range of values in a signed byte is -128 through $+127$. The decimal number 128 is 2^7, so the highest positive number that can be represented in seven bits is 01111111, or 127.[†]

Looking at even an eight-digit string of binary numbers is not all that easy, and when we get into larger numbers it is clear that writing them out in binary is cumbersome and error-prone. It is much more convenient to use a larger number system that is also an exact power of two. The first such system in common use was *octal*, or base 8 numbering. Each number in octal represents a

[†]Negative numbers use a special representation called two's-complement, which the arithmetic circuits can use more efficiently. See the Appendix for details.

group of three binary bits, and the eight digits from 0 through 7 cover all the possible combinations of three bits from 000 (0) through 111 (7). The binary number

011010101100

can be written in octal by first separating it into groups of three:

011 010 101 100

and then substituting the octal digit that matches each group:

3   2   5   4

Writing the binary number 011010101100 as 3254 makes it much easier to read and much less error-prone.

The problem with octal, however, is that we have by now settled on a byte as having eight digits, and we cannot separate eight bits into exact groups of three. The high-order (leftmost) octal digit represents two bits, not three, and this can be a source of confusion. Most binary numbers these days are therefore written in base 16 (which is 2^4), called *hexadecimal* or *hex*, where each hex digit is the equivalent of four binary digits. This allows us to describe the contents of a byte with exactly two hex digits with nothing short and nothing left over. The hex number system starts with the numbers 0 through 9, and uses the first six letters of the alphabet, A through F, for the remaining digits.[†] The binary number 01000101 becomes, in hex, 45:

4 = 0100, 5 = 0101, thus:
      01000101 → 0100 0101 → 4 5

[†]The Appendix includes a complete list of hex digits and their binary and decimal equivalents.

To convert this to decimal, we use the same technique shown earlier to describe decimal and binary numbers, only this time each position in the number is a power of 16:

$$5 \cdot 1 \ (16^0) = \ 5$$
$$4 \cdot 16 \ (16^1) = 64$$
$$= 69$$

Whether as a signed or unsigned number or as a character, whether represented in decimal, binary, octal, or hex, an eight-bit byte can still have only 256 possible values. When we need to work with a larger number, we instruct the computer to use two bytes in sequence and operate on them as a 16-bit *word*; the address of this word is the address of its first byte. Where a byte could hold 2^8 possibilities, a word can handle 2^{16}, or 65,536 different numbers. Combining four bytes into a single *longword* of 32 bits lets us work with 2^{32}, or four billion, possible values. One of the more common uses of a longword is to hold an address, which means that we have the capability (in theory, at least) of working with as much as four billion bytes of memory. On many machines we can use a *quadword* of four words (eight bytes) or 2^{64} bits, and sometimes even larger groupings. Quadwords and larger groups are not often used to hold integers, as there is seldom a use for numbers in the quadrillions. Instead, their most common purpose is as containers for *real numbers*, also known as *floating point numbers*.

An integer is a whole number: 1, −150, 69,734. It is mathematically correct to describe one integer as being "next to" another: 15 is next to 16, for example. Real numbers are integers combined with a fraction (even if the fraction is zero): 3.14159, 6.0, $3.1 \cdot 10^{43}$. No real number is "next to" another real number, for there is always some number in between (between 5.00001 and 5.00002 lies 5.000015, and so on, ad infinitum).

Real numbers are thus distinguished by having a decimal point. Because there is no way to dictate in advance how many digits will be to the left and to the right of the decimal point, a memory structure for real numbers must allow the decimal point to be anywhere among the string of digits—in other words, to "float" to any position. The real numbers .56743, 5.6743, 56.743, 5,674.3 and 56,743.0 are all possible values of a floating point number.

When a longword—a set of four bytes, or 32 bits—is used as a container for a floating point number, the range of numbers it can hold is (approximately) -10^{-38} to $+10^{38}$, an enormous spread. But it can still only hold four billion (2^{32}) specific numbers within that range, because that is all that can be represented by 32 binary bits. This means, among other things, that there will always be two real numbers that are in fact next to each other; at some point, the floating point number structure will be unable to describe those real numbers that fall between, say, 5.00000151 and 5.00000152. What is an absurdity in mathematics is, for the computer, a necessity. We can increase the precision—the maximum number of digits allowed to the right of the decimal point—by using larger groups of bytes (quadwords and octawords), but the number of digits is always finite; there is no way to represent infinity in memory. It is an example of what must always be borne in mind regarding the limitations inherent in any digital structure: It provides a *representation* of the real world, but never an exact analog. In most situations, the digital approximation is good enough (very few applications require a definition of π beyond the fifth decimal place). But it serves to remind us that not all data is within the computer's grasp.

One more type of memory structure remains to be discussed: the instruction itself. Every task that the computer circuitry carries out is determined, step by step, by binary codes residing in memory. Each instruction consists of one or more bytes in a sequence, beginning with an *op code* — a binary command to the computer — and as many parameters as may be required. The set of op codes makes up what is called the *machine language* of the computer — the language that all computer programs must ultimately be translated into in order for the computer to run them. This machine language is different for each type of computer, but for the sake of example let us define the HALT instruction (the instruction that shuts down the computer) as the binary op code 00000000 (in hex, 00). This simple instruction is one byte long, and consists solely of its op code.

Most instructions are more complex; for example, the binary op code 11010001 (hex "D1") might be an instruction to add two bytes together and store the result of the addition in a third

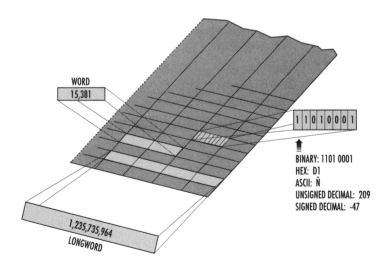

WORD
15,381

1 1 0 1 0 0 0 1

BINARY: 1101 0001
HEX: D1
ASCII: Ñ
UNSIGNED DECIMAL: 209
SIGNED DECIMAL: -47

1,235,735,964
LONGWORD

byte. The locations, or the addresses, of each of the bytes in question would immediately follow this op code as a set of three longwords; thus, the string of bytes containing these hex values:

D1 00 00 00 01 00 00 00 02 00 00 00 03

would be an instruction to the computer to add the contents of byte 00000001 to the contents of byte 00000002, and store the result in byte 00000003.

Modern programmers do not, of course, write programs in machine language nor do they determine the physical addresses of data. This will be explained in Part III; for the moment the point is that the op code actually defines for the computer the particular construction of memory. A byte containing "D1" might be an unsigned number (decimal 209), a signed number (decimal −47), a character (ASCII Ñ), one of several bytes making up a floating point number, or, as in this case, the op code part of an instruction. The computer knows that is an instruction because its circuits are currently describing this location as the next instruction to execute; it knows that it is to treat the data in locations 00000001, 00000002, and 00000003 as bytes because the op code "D1" means "add three bytes." The op code "D2" might instruct the computer to add three words, "D3" to add three longwords, "D4" to add floating point longwords, and so on.

Other op codes use the address part of the instruction to point to another instruction rather than to data; for example, if the op code "41" means "branch if greater," then the instruction

41 0A 45 89 FC

will direct the computer to continue execution with the instruction at location 0A4589FC (to "branch" or "jump") if the result of the most recent arithmetic operation was greater than zero.

There is always the danger that the address this instruction points to is data rather than program; for that matter, "41" is also the ASCII code for the character "A," and it is possible that the computer wandered into a string of text by mistake and is now trying to execute it. When this happens, the circuits will almost certainly detect an impossible condition such as an address outside of memory or an illegal instruction code (only privileged programs are allowed to execute the HALT instruction, for example) and abort the program. In addition, many computers now divide memory into program space and data space, and will not permit a branch instruction to jump into data. Modern programming languages also provide methods for minimizing the chances of such an error occurring. Still, memory, with all its power and flexibility, remains a stage full of traps for the unwary. Part III examines some of the techniques programmers use to guard against misuse of memory.

7

"ON A CLEAR DISK

YOU CAN SEEK FOREVER"

What we call "memory" in a computer is not really an exact analog to human memory. Computer memory is relatively small and expensive, is designed to be constantly changing, and loses its contents when the power is turned off. A better analogy might be to compare it to consciousness: Just as we remember many things but are currently conscious of only a few of them at any given time, so the computer memory, or "consciousness," contains only those instructions and data that the computer is currently working on. The rest of what in a person would be called "memory" must reside elsewhere in the computer, on some *mass storage device*.

Mass storage devices are the computer equivalent of those memories of which we are not currently aware. They hold programs and data that may at some point be needed for a computer operation, but not right at this moment. All computers (with the exception of specialized microprocessors) use some sort of mass storage, the most common types being tapes and disks; CD-ROMs and other optical disks are also standard today. Magnetic tapes have been in use the longest; these are long strips of plastic that have been coated with a magnetic surface. A tape drive's write-head will put information onto the tape as a series of binary bits by setting or reversing the magnetic polarity, while its read-head will scan the tape and pick up data as a series of magnetic signals. Large amounts of data can be stored on a tape this way. And since the value of the data is determined by the polarity of a magnetized bit of iron rather than by the presence or absence of an electric current, the data is not dependent on a power source, but is permanent until it is changed by another magnetic operation.

However, tapes are *sequential* devices; in order to read a piece of information stored at a spot 500 feet from the start of the tape, it is necessary to read the intervening 499 feet first. This means that while a tape is useful as an archival tool, it is of limited use when the computer needs random items of information right away.

The most common *random access* mass storage device is the *disk*. A disk consists of one or more platters which have been coated with a magnetic surface similar to that of a tape. But unlike a tape, a disk is constructed so that a computer can access any part of it at any time. It can do this because the platters are divided into separate tracks. There is a read/write-head for each platter mounted on a moveable arm, and a disk drive mechanism moves this arm in or out, in what is called a "seek" operation, to locate the desired track. (Some disk drives are fixed-head; that is, they have a read/write-head permanently mounted over each cylinder. This provides faster access by eliminating seek time, but is more expensive.) Some disks are removable; others are not. A removable disk is useful for keeping a copy of valuable data in some place other than on the computer, while a fixed disk is generally larger and faster.

Compact disk (CD) devices use a reflective medium that responds to light instead of magnetism, and reads the data by means of a laser rather than a magnetized read/write-head, but it too accesses the data in random order. Until recently, the only way to get information onto a CD was with expensive factory equipment, which still made them useful for storing large amounts of permanent data such as an encyclopedia or a multimedia game. Writable CDs are now starting to come on the market, and eventually CDs and other types of optical disks may replace magnetic disks, since they are not vulnerable to stray magnetic impulses.

Whether using an optical CD or a magnetic disk, one can access any part of it at any time; therefore these devices can—and must—organize their contents differently from a sequential tape. To begin with, each group of bits on a disk has a unique address, in much the same way as each byte in memory has its own address. However, in the case of a disk these bit groups are larger. While the exact size of a *sector*—the smallest unit of data that can be addressed on a disk—may vary from one computer type to another, in general a sector will be 256 or 512 bytes in size. When the CPU reads in data from the disk or writes data out to it, it does so in transfers of one or more sectors at a time.

Since each sector has its own address, we can tie a group of related sectors together by maintaining a list of their addresses. A collection of sectors grouped together is called a *file*; for example, all the sectors on my disk that together contain the text of this chapter constitute this chapter's file.

A file is at the boundary point between the internal disk organization and its appearance to the outside world. As users, and even for the most part as programmers, we are not particularly concerned with the internal layout of disk data, and the address of a specific sector is meaningless to us. However, a file is a

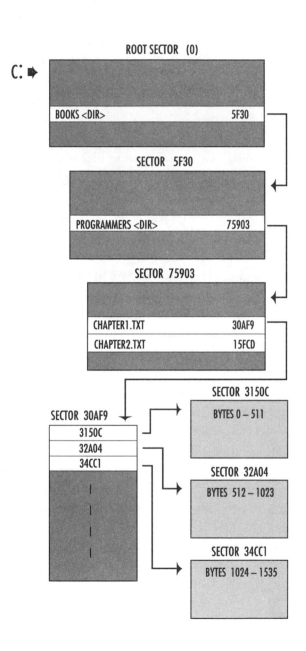

meaningful collection of data, and its meaning is made clear if we designate it by name rather than by number. The disk controller, on the other hand, cannot locate a sector on the disk by name, only by its hexadecimal address. So we construct a *directory*, a list of file names combined with the addresses of their corresponding sectors. And since the directory must itself be a file, it too is stored as a name in some higher directory, which, being itself a file, has an entry in some still higher directory.

Eventually there must come an end to this chain. By convention, a designated sector — generally sector 0 — is set aside to contain the list of sector addresses that make up the first directory on the disk, which is the *root directory*. Once this starting point is known, it is possible to walk down the directory chain and locate the proper file by name and locate its sectors.

File names will vary from manufacturer to manufacturer, but they all follow certain conventions. First, they are limited in length, whether it be six, eight, or thirty-one characters; there is only so much room that can be set aside in a directory sector. Second, file names can only use certain characters, such as alphabetical (A–Z) and numeric (0–9) characters. Most systems also allow a few special characters such as a dash (-) or underscore (_). In the beginning (and on some computers even today) a filename alone was used, but it quickly became clear that some sort of file description would be useful as well. A filename *extension*, usually three to fifteen characters, has become standard as well, and certain extensions have achieved an almost universal conventionality. For example, an executable program will use the extension EXE, while DIR identifies a directory.† Data files are often DAT, while a text file (which is a special kind of data file)

---

† On most PCs, directory files are identified by a special code indicating file type rather than by an extension, but the principle is the same. Some directory programs display a

may be labeled TXT. Certain extensions are required, while others are left to the discretion of the programmer or user.

From the point of view of the user, then, the location of a file is not some incomprehensible hexadecimal address, but a directory name or series of directory and subdirectory names, followed by the filename and extension. When the name of the device itself is included, then the complete description is referred to as a *path*—for example, this chapter is stored on my computer as C:\BOOKS\PROGRAMMER\CHAPTER7.TXT. The computer looks up "BOOKS" in the root directory for disk device C, then finds "PROGRAMMER" in the BOOKS directory, and finally looks in the PROGRAMMER subdirectory of BOOKS for the file CHAPTER7.TXT.

This is one of those places where it is necessary to point out that there are many ways of doing the same thing, and they will vary considerably depending on what type of computer is actually being used. The form I have just used is common on many personal computers; on a DEC VAX, the same file path would be C: [BOOKS.PROGRAMMER] CHAPTER7.TXT. These variations exist because each computer uses its own type of operating system, a basic program that controls how all other programs use the computer hardware. The hardware of the computer, while it is capable of many things on its own, is not capable of locating a file on a disk by name. Like the disk drive, it only knows about numbers. Only a program such as an operating system can make sense out of file name ABCDEF.EXE and perform the machine instructions that locate it on the disk. Indeed, without an operating system, there would be no way to use the computer at all.

---

description of the extension rather than the extension itself; for example, the file PROGRAM.EXE might appear on the directory listing as "PROGRAM: Executable file."

8

A BRIEF INTERRUPTION

Before proceeding to a discussion of operating systems, one more facet of the hardware needs to be discussed: the interrupt. Each computer circuit performs one operation at a time. This means that while the CPU is executing an instruction to add two numbers, it cannot execute any other instruction (although it can be looking ahead and setting up for the next one). But just because the CPU's instruction circuits are tied up with an operation, it does not mean that all its other circuits must sit idly by.

In the early days of computers, however, they did just that. For example, the IBM 1620 (built in 1959), a computer of which I have fond memories, had a control panel which included a disk interlock light. Whenever the computer was reading from or writing to its disk, the light would go on to reassure the watcher that the computer had not crashed; it was merely waiting for the disk operation to finish so it could move on to the next instruction.

But even on a machine as slow as a 1620 (a machine so slow that I could tell from watching the light patterns when it was doing a multiply!), many machine instructions could have been executed in the time it took to read from or write to a disk, much less any other input/output operation, and it quickly became apparent to computer designers that making the whole computer wait for the disk or the keyboard or the printer was a tremendous waste of valuable computer time.

The solution was to start an input/output (I/O) operation and let it run by itself while the computer went on to execute other instructions in the program. (A modern computer can execute several million machine instructions in the time it takes to complete a single disk transfer.) When the read or write operation was finished, the I/O circuitry would *interrupt* the central processing unit, letting it know that the requested data was now in memory (for input) or that the output had completed and the output device was now ready for the next operation. Thus, if a program has other work to do while waiting for a user to type in a command or data on the keyboard, it can do that work while it waits; when the user has something to say and hits a key, that will cause an interrupt to occur so the program can process it. If the program has nothing to do, it can go to sleep, and when the interrupt occurs it will wake the program up again.

The computer's internal clock can also be set to interrupt the computer at specified intervals (say, every millisecond — every thousandth of a second); a special program responds to these interrupts by counting them. At every thousandth interrupt, it will update the clock display to the next second. And when a specified number of milliseconds have been counted, it may take other actions, such as initiating a new program. This is one way in which a microwave microprocessor, for example, can be programmed to turn off the heating element when fifteen minutes have elapsed.

But what works well for a dedicated microprocessor is still too inefficient for a general-purpose computer capable of running many different programs for different users at the same time. While one program is waiting for input from a disk or keyboard, the CPU should be executing the instructions of another program that needs to do internal calculations on data it has already received. But it is too much to expect a program to have to worry about passing control to another program every time it waits for some external event; programs are complicated enough as it is without being asked to deal with this extra overhead. Nor should that other program have to depend on the kindness of strangers who may not know (or care) that the second program is waiting. An overall controlling program is needed to manage the resources of the computer and see that they are shared equitably. Operating systems are the programs that fill this need.

9

OPERATING SYSTEMS

Early programmers not only had to contend with the complexities of bits, bytes, and longwords, they also had to write code to handle all the administrative tasks as well. If a program needed information from the disk, the programmer had to know the number of the sector where it resided, or how to find that sector number, and had to code the actual instructions to get the information. If a program was supposed to send its results to a printer, the programmer was responsible for setting up and formatting the line and for writing the actual machine code to send the line to the printer, advance the paper to the next line, and so on.

This proved to be a tedious business, as one might easily imagine. Not only that, but each new program needed a whole new set of the same code to do the same thing as the previous one. While it is possible to create a library of such programs (subroutines) that can be included with the main program, it soon became clear that it would be easier and more efficient for the programmers to have a centralized program to take care of I/O devices and perform other administrative or "housekeeping" chores.

With the advent of interrupts, it also became possible—indeed, highly desirable—to keep several programs around in various states of execution, and let one use the CPU while the others were waiting for input or output to complete. But it was impractical for the programmers to design each program so that it would know how to cooperate with any others that might (or might not) be running at the same time, so once again a centralized program was needed to organize the computer's resources and make sure that they were properly shared by the various programs that needed them. Such programs are now known as *operating systems*.

An operating system is the one program on a computer that is always running. It is the program that runs when the computer first starts up; there are hardware circuits that load the startup (*boot*) section of the operating system from a predefined location, such as sector 0001 of the disk, and execute it. (This procedure is often called "booting up" the computer.) It is the program that controls all the others, deciding which ones will run and when, which resources (terminals, disk files, modems, CPU time) each program will get, and for how long. If a resource such as a disk, printer, or memory needs to be shared, it is the operating system that makes sure that the sharing is done cleanly so that no program interferes with another. When two programs reside in memory, for example, they are each restricted to that part of memory which the operating system has allocated to them.

The operating system is the program that responds to interrupts from the clock and all other I/O devices. It decides which program is scheduled to run next, and which program is supposed to process the input that was just received from a terminal or a disk or a modem. It is the program that takes a file name and looks it up in the directory structure, and the program that creates those files on the disk. It starts all the other programs and cleans up after them when they exit cleanly or when they *abort*—that is, when they have some error that causes them to fail.[†]

In a typical scenario, a user will issue a command to the operating system to run a desired program—for example, a word processing program. The operating system will locate the program on the disk directory, assign space in memory for the program to use, load the program (or part of it) into memory, and transfer control to that program. From time to time, the word processing program will make requests back to the operating system, such as asking it to look up a file on the disk and to read in a piece of it, send some text to the printer, or suspend the program until the user types a character on the keyboard. In addition, the operating system will monitor the amount of time the program has been active (by counting interrupts from the clock) and every so often will suspend the operation of the current program in order to give other programs a chance to run for a while.

There are three basic ways in which operating systems arrange for these programs to run: batch processing, interactive, and real-time. *Batch processing* is the oldest technique for passing programs through a computer. The term dates back to the days when

---

[†]Operating systems, being themselves programs written by human beings, have also been known to fail. Because there is no other program to clean up after them, an operating system failure generally results in a complete failure of the entire computer, otherwise known as a "system crash." The only way to recover from such a situation is to reboot the computer all over again.

users would write their programs on punched cards and submit them to a computer operator. The operator would collect the programs in a "batch" and run them all through the computer's card reader. The computer would read in as many programs at a time as it had room for, convert them to machine language, and execute them, printing the results out on the high-speed printer, after which the operator would bundle the printout and the cards together and return them to the user. In a busy computer center, it might take a day or more for the user to get the results of such an exercise, and of course if there were any errors or changes, the user would have to go through the whole process all over again.

Such a situation was (barely) tolerable only as long as computer time was seen as more valuable than programmer and user time, a condition which was definitely no longer true by around 1970. As computer hardware became more common and manufacturing became more standardized, hardware prices dropped dramatically; at the same time, programs were becoming more sophisticated and their users more demanding, leading to an ever-increasing demand for ever more expensive programming talent. Idle programmers and frustrated users prompted the growth of another type of computer processing: interactive.

In *interactive processing* (also known as *time-sharing*, though the two terms are not quite identical), a user "interacts" directly with the computer, generally through a terminal—a keyboard and monitor combination. The user connects to the computer (often simply a matter of turning the terminal on), goes through an identification procedure if necessary (another operating system function), and from then on enters typed commands to the operating system to perform various desired tasks. These tasks may be performed by programs that are part of the operating system (such as a directory lookup), packaged programs such as word processors, or programs that the users themselves have written and are now trying to run. All of these programs interact with the user through the terminal; whenever the user types a key, the operating system, responding to an interrupt signal, picks up the character that was entered and passes it on to the running program. While the user is choosing the next key, the operating system is doing the same thing for the other users who are also on the system at that moment. Every user seems to be the only person on the computer, but in reality hundreds may be sharing it (hence the term "time-sharing"). The appearance of being the sole user is the result of the vast difference between computer speed and the human perception of time; the computer handles each user request so rapidly that we often do not notice it is processing other users' programs as well.

Operating systems tend to have a bias toward one or the other of these two modes. On most DEC computers, for example, the entire orientation is toward interactive processing, with batch jobs running on a kind of virtual terminal. On the other hand, the most popular IBM mainframe operating system, MVS, is totally batch-oriented. Time-sharing users are connected to a subsystem called TSO, which runs as a batch job with no time limit.

Real-time processing is a variation of interactive processing, where a program is controlling devices other than a user terminal, and must respond to them within a certain period of time. An automated factory is a good example: As each part moves along the conveyor belt, the computer has only a few seconds to work on it before it slips out of range. This gives such a program a greater sense of urgency than the ordinary interactive program, which will wait patiently for a human being to make a move. While technically it is the program rather than the operating system that must respond in real time, such programs function with the cooperation of the operating system, and so deserve a category of their own.

Which particular mode of processing is used depends primarily on the purpose of the program. Interactive processing is the most common, and PCs use it almost exclusively, but batch processing is still the norm on many mainframes, where it makes the most efficient use of the computer for running programs that do not need input from a human being. A report of daily activities is a good example: The report program is scheduled to run at midnight, gathering data stored in the course of the day from disk files, and produces a printed report. No live person need be involved (or even notice the operation) until the printout is done. Batch processing is a good way to handle such jobs that are scheduled in advance, as well as other jobs that a user may interactively request but has no need to see in operation.

All three modes may be used in combination in a complex environment. At an airport ticket counter, the clerk types in the passenger's name and flight information on a terminal running in interactive mode; the program receives the typed information, immediately performs its database lookups, and responds by printing out the boarding pass. At the same time, it adds an item in the file that will later be used by a batch job to print out the passenger list. When the clerk puts the passenger's baggage on the conveyor belt to be loaded onto the plane, another program running in real time follows its progress and directs it to the proper bin.[†]

The operating system also protects programs from mistakes .

[†]Or so one hopes. The difficulties of real-time programming are illustrated by the problems Denver's new airport has been having with its automated baggage handling system. For a while, the airport's informal slogan was: "We hope you're going to Fargo, because your luggage is!"

that other programs might make by performing certain actions on their behalf, and thus controlling which programs are affected by them. Input/output (I/O), in particular, is an area where a program can easily overstep its bounds. Ordinary programs do not perform dangerous tasks such as I/O themselves, but instead make requests to the operating system to do so by means of special machine instructions called *system services*. These include such obvious calls as requests to read a character from a terminal or write a line to the printer, or to look up a file in the disk directory. But operating systems offer a whole range of services such as reporting the current time, expanding the program's memory allocation, starting up other programs, and making entries in the administrator's log files. In each case, the operating system will determine if the program (more precisely, the program's user) has the privilege to perform the operation, and then either grants or denies the request.

An operating system has the power to control these other programs because it runs in a privileged mode that allows it to do things such as the actual input and output operations, setting of regions of memory, starting and stopping programs, and so on. A classic example of a privileged operation is the HALT instruction, something no ordinary program should ever be allowed to do. If such a program tried it, the protections built into the hardware would reject the attempt and instead alert the operating system (by means of yet another interrupt signal called a *trap*) that the program has attempted to execute an illegal instruction.[†] A sim-

---

[†] In many computers, op code "00" is deliberately designated as the HALT instruction. This is because data space is often initialized to zero, and unused code areas are often set to zero as well. If the program is caught—trapped—attempting to execute a "00" op code, it usually means that it wandered into the wrong part of memory by mistake, not that some malicious programmer attempted to shut down the machine.

ilar type of interrupt occurs when the program tries to access a location outside its assigned region of memory. The operating system then informs the user that the program has trapped and will, in general, abort the execution. Most such violations are of course inadvertent, and in fact memory access violations are one of the most common programming errors.

Some programs, however, may really need to do some of the privileged operations. A specialized program to run an unusual device that is outside the standard repertoire is one example. Modern operating systems offer complex mixes of privileges and security arrangements that are tied to the particular user who wants to use them. For this reason, all users start their sessions (whether batch or interactive) on such an operating system by identifying themselves in some way, and prove their identity by means of a password or other secret code.[†] They are then granted the privileges and accesses associated with their identification, and the programs they run can now request and sometimes even directly perform certain restricted operations.

It is here that the weakness of the personal computer is exposed. Because it began as an esoteric curiosity for expert hobbyists, the PC does not have a restricted set of op codes nor many guards against misuse. The early computers were so small, so inaccessible, and so arcane, it was assumed that anyone who was willing to spend the time and energy to make one work was knowledgeable and would in fact resent the safeguards that protect lesser mortals from their own folly. These programmers developed the bad habit of assuming that the whole computer was theirs to play with, and many of their programs were constantly stepping on each other as they fought for control of interrupts

---

[†] Fingerprint and retina scans are not yet in common use, but soon they may be.

and pieces of memory. If most programs sold for the PC today cooperate with each other and with the PC's operating system, it is only because their writers have learned discipline on their own, not because the hardware requires them to do so.

If a programmer deliberately takes advantage of this vulnerability and refuses to cooperate voluntarily, the result will often be a computer virus. The openness and flexibility that the early independent users of the PC prized so highly is the same quality that makes the PC so much more vulnerable to malicious programming than its larger cousins. Recently, new personal computers have come on the market with hardware features that can be used to bring some order to this chaos, but the operating systems that can take advantage of them are still being written, and even when they are available there will still be millions of vulnerable computers out there for a long time to come.[†]

It should be clear from the preceding discussion that the operating system is far more closely tied to a particular hardware than is any other program. Most operating systems are in fact written by the manufacturer of the computer and sold together with it as a package, although in some cases competing software companies will offer alternative operating systems, and in the case of the personal computer, manufacturers of IBM-type PCs have relied completely on an outside vendor, Microsoft, to supply the operating system.[‡] This combination of operating system and computer hardware is called a *platform*, and every program stands, as it were, on some platform in order to run. But

---

[†]This is not to say that these new computers will be invulnerable; all computers and their operating systems have weaknesses that a malicious programmer can exploit. But it will not be as easy as it used to be.

[‡]Microsoft has actually produced at least three operating systems for the IBM PC and its clones: MS-DOS, Windows 95, and Windows NT.

while a program that works on one platform may not work on another, the basic programming techniques themselves are not dependent on the particular system or computer. Whether for microprocessor or mainframe, all programs are built using certain fundamental tools: the common principles of programming.

Part III

FUNDAMENTAL

TOOLS OF

PROGRAMMING

10

THE LANGUAGE OF THE MACHINE

All computers speak only in binary. Thus, an instruction in memory consists of an op code — 11000000, say — and zero or more operands, also in binary, describing the locations or the values to be operated on. A computer circuit designer will more or less arbitrarily assign a number to the different instructions the machine is capable of, and the set of these numbers becomes the *machine language*. For example, 11000000 could mean "add two longwords," while 11000010 is the op code for "subtract two longwords." If the first longword starts at byte 0110010111001010 — its address in memory in binary form — and the second longword has a starting address of 1101001101100100, then the binary instruction

11000000 0110010111001010 1101001101100100

means "add the number in the longword at the first location to the number in the longword in the second location, and store the result in the second location."

Obviously, writing whole programs using binary is an impossible task, and even if we group them together into octal for the sake of convenience, that string of numbers—014 014 562 551 544—is still cumbersome and awkward.

Yet, the earliest programmers did just that—they wrote their programs in octal.[†] To make life a little easier for themselves, they developed mnemonic equivalents for the binary op codes and would make notes using those mnemonics to help them keep track of the programs they were trying to develop. Thus, "A" would stand for "Add," and when the programmer was ready to prepare the machine code for the computer to read, the appropriate binary (or octal) op code for "A" would be substituted.

Maurice Wilkes, who was project director for the EDSAC computer at Cambridge, England, is credited with being the first to realize that the computer could be made to do the job of translating "A" to its binary machine code equivalent. In October 1948, he assigned his research student, David Wheeler, to come up with a program to convert these mnemonics into computer instructions. Wheeler's program, Initial Orders, consisted of just thirty machine instructions and ranks as the first assembler (Campbell-Kelly and Aspray 1996, 184).

An *assembler* is the name given to a type of computer program that reads in lines of text with each line describing one machine instruction by means of mnemonics and symbols. It was an advance made possible by the use of the stored-program computer, in which one program could read in another program written in human-readable *source code*—the lines of text—and convert it to

---

[†]Grace Hopper once commented that she became so immersed in octal that she would occasionally use octal arithmetic when making entries in her checkbook. As a result, it was out of balance for three months until her brother, a banker, figured out what she had been doing (Hopper 1981, 7).

a program meaningful to the computer. The binary machine code that was the output of the first program would then be loaded into memory as the new program to be executed.

The first assembler only eased the burden of remembering the binary op codes; programmers still had to assign memory locations to the data elements, and since these locations might move every time the program was modified, they would carefully have to reassign all the data addresses each time. Similarly, if a program instruction said to go to a specific location in the program under a certain condition, that location, too, would have to be corrected every time a new instruction was added to the program.

To illustrate what I mean, let us consider a hypothetical machine (and to make things easier, the machine will use decimal rather than binary). The machine's memory has 10,000 bytes that have addresses in the range 0000 through 9999. Each byte can contain a decimal number in the range 00 through 99. Thus, two consecutive bytes are used to hold an address. (Remember that bytes in sequential order can be combined to form larger units.)

On this machine, let us have these decimal op codes, each of which fits into one byte:

00   STOP the machine;
01   READ in a number from the keyboard;
02   ADD two numbers together (storing the answer in the second number); and
03   DISPLAY a number on the screen.

The machine instruction STOP does not need any operands, so the entire STOP instruction is one byte long—it consists only of the op code. The DISPLAY and READ instructions each require one byte for the op code and two bytes for the address of the data they are operating on; thus, these instructions are each three bytes in length. Similarly, the ADD instruction, which uses two memory addresses, is five bytes long. Finally, let us state that the READ, ADD, and DISPLAY instructions all work with data in the range 0 through 99,999,999 — in other words, they operate on four bytes (or a longword) of data.

Now let us write a simple machine language program to read in two numbers, add them, and display the result. I would start by making notes using mnemonics:

> READ first
> READ second
> ADD first to second
> DISPLAY second
> STOP
> first: longword
> second: longword

The next step would be to write the same instructions in binary, so that they can be punched onto the paper tape. I will also make a note of where each instruction is to be placed in memory by jotting down its address (or the address of the first byte of the instruction) to the left of a colon:

> 0000: 01 xx xx
> 0003: 01 xx xx
> 0006: 02 xx xx xx xx
> 0011: 03 xx xx
> 0014: 00
> 0015: xx xx xx xx
> 0019: xx xx xx xx

The address part of the instructions contain "xx" at this point, because I have not figured out where the data is to be located.

Once I have placed all the instructions in their proper locations in memory, I can count the number of bytes used by the program. I then place my data in the bytes following the last instruction of the program (byte 0014): FIRST will start at byte 0015, and the address of the first byte of SECOND will be 0019. (Each data element is a longword, and thus takes up four bytes.) The final program as it is to be punched on the paper tape now looks like this:

```
01 00 15
01 00 19
02 00 15 00 19
03 00 19
00
```

The Initial Orders program made this task just slightly easier, since I would only have to write:

```
READ 0115
READ 0119
ADD 0115 0119
DISPLAY 0119
STOP
```

and the assembler would do the conversions instead.

But I still have to figure out the addresses of the data space myself. And if I make any changes to the program—if I want to read in and add a third number as well—I would have to recalculate all the addresses all over again.

But if an assembler can convert mnemonic op codes to binary, it can also keep track of addresses and use them when necessary as well. An assembly programmer assigns a symbol—a *label*—to a location in the program or data area; the assembler then associates that symbol with the value of the current location, and whenever that symbol is used the assembler substitutes the correct address for it. If the program changed, we would simply run the changed source code through the assembler, creating a new version of the machine code with new addresses. My hypothetical program is now written as:

```
START:    READ FIRST
          READ SECOND
          ADD FIRST, SECOND
          DISPLAY SECOND
          STOP
FIRST:    LONGWORD
SECOND:   LONGWORD
          END START
```

The label START is associated with the first location of the first instruction, and the labels FIRST and SECOND are associated with longwords at the end of the program. END START tells the assembler that this is the last line of the source code, and also that the program will start at START. If the program has to be changed to add three numbers, all that is necessary is to change the source code to:

```
START:    READ FIRST
          READ SECOND
          READ THIRD
          ADD FIRST, SECOND
          ADD SECOND, THIRD
          DISPLAY THIRD
          STOP
FIRST:    LONGWORD
SECOND:   LONGWORD
```

THIRD: LONGWORD
           END START

This new version of the program, once assembled, will perform the new task. The assembler has taken over the drudge work of calculating the addresses as well as putting in the binary op codes.

As much an advance as assembly languages represented over pure binary code, they still required a detailed, sophisticated knowledge of the machine. The programmer also had to be aware of every action and side effect, had to worry about registers and accumulators and the sizes of the data fields. Moreover, each type of computer had its own set of binary op codes and thus its own assembly language, and while the principles might be similar, the languages were totally different. Where one machine might use a single MOVE instruction to transfer a piece of data from one location to another, another might take two instructions to do the same thing: LOAD and STORE. Not only could a program not be moved from one computer to another, a programmer, no matter how proficient in one computer's assembly language, would have to learn a whole new set of instructions and other details before being able to write the simplest program on an unfamiliar machine.

As soon as computers began to grow large enough to contain programs more than a few pages in length, it became apparent that the detailed demands of assembly programming were creating a major strain on programmer resources, and interest developed in finding ways to have the computer produce what was at first called "automatic programming." The idea was that a computer program would be able to accept statements in some form of a higher level than assembly language, and turn them into machine code while automatically taking care of the housekeeping details such as data movement in and out of arithmetic accumulators, assignment of registers, and so forth. Such programs, originally known as translators, soon became universally known as *compilers*,[†] and this class of languages as *high-level languages*. The first compilers produced code that usually worked but was extremely inefficient, and most programmers were completely convinced that no translating program could ever produce machine code as efficiently as an assembly programmer.

Then, in late 1953, John Backus persuaded IBM to let him try to come up with a new compiler technique that could easily translate high-level language into efficient code. In 1957, Backus and his team delivered the first commercially successful high-level language: FORTRAN.

FORTRAN was originally designed for use on the IBM 704, which was the first machine to use hardware floating point instructions. (On previous machines, programmers had emulated floating point arithmetic by using a series of integer instructions.) The name FORTRAN stands for "FORmula TRANslation," and the language was primarily focused on converting mathematical formulas into computer instructions. As such, it could be used by physicists, chemists, and other scientists, who could not be expected to take the considerable time and effort to master machine and assembly code. A typical line of text in a FORTRAN program might be:

A = (x * 2) / Y

which is read as "A equals X times 2, divided by Y." That one line of source code above might produce these machine instruc-

---

[†]Grace Hopper gets the credit for coming up with the term "compiler," although her first effort, the A-O compiler for the UNIVAC in 1953, was far too slow to be usable (Campbell-Kelly and Aspray 1996, 187).

tions, with the compiler assigning floating point register FR1 for the task:

```
LOAD   FR1,X
MULF   FR1,#2.0
DIVF   FR1,Y
STORE  FR1,A†
```

This snippet of code is not intended to be a real example (real ones are even more complicated), but only an illustration of the sort of drudge work that programmers had to deal with when writing in assembly language, from which the FORTRAN compiler had now spared them.

FORTRAN, for all its advantages over assembly language, was not really suited for many of the tasks computers were being asked to do. It did not handle large data structures very well, nor was it easy to write programs in it that produced neatly laid-out reports. In other words, it was not really suited for the needs of the business community—the insurance companies, banks, and other corporations that were the major purchasers of these large machines.

While a number of languages attempted to address this need, the one that became most popular was COBOL, or COmmon Business Oriented Language. One of the reasons for COBOL's success is that, unlike FORTRAN, COBOL's designers were primarily concerned with data representation and with file and record manipulation. In COBOL, for example, a programmer can write instructions to access a file of bank deposits, locate an individual customer's account, and produce a neatly formatted re-

---

†Assume that arithmetic must be performed in a register—an arithmetic accumulator—and that MULF and DIVF are "multiply floating point" and "divide floating point," respectively.

port for managers to use—all by using commands that are part of the language.

Another factor was that unlike FORTRAN, COBOL was developed by an independent organization instead of a specific manufacturer, and one of its primary design objectives was to be able to write programs in a language that would work identically (or nearly so) on many different machines. Customers very much wanted to have a single standard language instead of the multitude of incompatible languages then being offered by the different manufacturers. But the computer industry was concerned about possible charges of antitrust violations if the manufacturers cooperated too closely on one language. In coordination with the Department of Defense, therefore, the various computer manufacturers established the Committee on Data Systems and Languages (CODASYL), and under its aegis produced the specifications for COBOL 60. The Pentagon's purchasing office then announced that it would only buy or lease computers that had a COBOL compiler, unless the manufacturer could demonstrate that its computer was better off without one. No one bothered to try. And even though the federal government no longer insists on having COBOL, it is still the most widely used language in business programming today.

COBOL also attempts to mimic natural language, the idea being that a program should be easy to read (ease of writing was a lesser consideration). The COBOL equivalent of the FORTRAN statement A = (x * 2) / Y would be:

> MULTIPLY X by 2 giving TEMP
> DIVIDE TEMP by Y giving A[†]

[†]There was a major argument among the early designers of COBOL between those who wanted to code arithmetic operations using only the COBOL verb structure (ADD, SUBTRACT, MULTIPLY, and DIVIDE) and those who insisted that

However, the more common sort of COBOL statement would be something like

SUBTRACT COST FROM PRICE GIVING PROFIT

which was the sort of instruction that managers and executives could at least pretend to understand. This provided an added "comfort factor" that helped to make the language popular among those who paid the bills, even if programmers sometimes found it too verbose.

Although from a programmer's perspective these and similar high-level languages represented an improvement over machine and assembly language, their syntax nonetheless did not lend themselves to ease of use. Programmers would often use tricks and shortcuts, and what one programmer wrote was often hard for another programmer to understand. COBOL, FORTRAN, and other similar languages were, simply put, inelegant.

The lack of consideration for the aesthetic qualities of a language is more than a matter of academic prejudice; it is dangerous.[†] As programming projects grew more complex, teams of programmers working together became the norm. Each programmer not only had to understand what the others were doing, but

---

programmers should have the flexibility to write mathematical equations in COBOL as well (Sammet 1981, 220). The compromise solution was to include the COMPUTE verb, so that these two statements, for example, could also be written as

COMPUTE A = (X * 2) / Y

However, unless the programmer is very careful in setting up the data descriptions, the results of a COMPUTE statement may not be precisely predictable.

[†]Computer scientists have often professed disdain for COBOL for a variety of reasons, among them that it is "ugly." Shneiderman (1987, 419) argues that a large part of their pique has to do with the subject of most COBOL programs—business data processing problems which are simply not that interesting to academics with a mathematical orientation. However, he too admits that there are serious flaws in the COBOL design, particularly in the earlier versions.

also had to be careful not to interfere with anyone else's data. Languages such as FORTRAN and COBOL, with their undifferentiated use of data and their inelegant syntax, did not make this job any easier.

A number of computer experts from the United States and Europe, including John Backus, the inventor of FORTRAN, met over the years from 1957 to 1962 to formulate a language that would deal with some of these issues. The result was ALGOL 60, the first structured programming language. ALGOL 60 is not used much anymore, although it and its successor, ALGOL 68, were popular in Europe for many years. The language definition contains obscurities and ambiguities that have never been completely resolved, and some of its data restrictions are considered onerous by other language designers.†

However, ALGOL did establish the fundamental principles of structured programming, which later languages have since refined.

The goal of structured programming is to write programs that can be proven correct. This is possible (at least in theory) because in a structured program we should always be able to tell, while reading the code, where we are at any given point in the execution of the program, as well as how we got there and where in the program we go next. While this has become something of a holy grail that may never be achieved in practice, programs written in languages designed using structured programming principles are in general easier to follow and easier to fix. Such languages are also simpler in form, relying on library routines rather than attempting to build functionality into the language definition. For example, the C language has only thirty-five key-

---

†See, for example, Knuth (1987, 61–68) and Wegner (1987, 7).

words (reserved terms that are part of the language such as "if" and "long") while COBOL 85 has more than 350—not just basic words like "COMPUTE" and "ADD," but also detailed operations such as "SORT," "REWRITE," "INSPECT," and "GENERATE."

Another goal of structured programming is to provide a means of writing large programs in many pieces with minimal coordination and yet still have the pieces fit together. While it is possible to do all this in languages such as FORTRAN or COBOL, or even in assembly languages, these languages are not designed to encourage structured code, and neither guard against violations of structured principles nor prevent data corruption. These are the principles and issues that the next few chapters will explore.

11

FORMS OF DATA DEFINITION

The chapter on memory described the various ways in which the same memory locations can be used to hold different types of data. In all those cases, the physical data is actually nothing more than a sequence of binary bits; the meaning of these bits depends entirely on which machine instructions operate on them. Instructions such as "move characters," "increment byte," or "store floating point," respectively, will describe the objects of their manipulations as a string of characters, a signed byte, and a floating point longword. When writing in assembly language, the programmer selects the appropriate instruction for each such data type. In high-level languages, the compiler will make the selection, and so the programmer must provide guidance in some way.

How this is done will, of course, vary from language to language, but there are certain conceptual points that almost all such languages have in common. One of these is the idea of the *variable.* A variable is a location in memory set aside to hold data that may change in the course of the program execution. The variable is defined by giving it a name according to the rules of the computer language. Once defined, the variable name (or label, or symbol—the terms are often interchangeable) is used consistently, throughout the program or section of the program, as meaning that particular location and the type of data that location contains. If, for example, I define three variables:[†]

integer A
float B, C

then whenever I use any of them in an operation statement, the compiler will generate the appropriate machine code: integer and floating point arithmetic instructions, respectively. If I combine them, as in:

C = A + B

then, depending on the language, the compiler will either generate instructions to convert the contents of A to a floating point number before adding it to B, or else will mark it as a semantic error.[††]

If I mean to use a symbol for its value, I must use it in a different form—as a *constant*. A constant, unlike a variable, associates the label with a value rather than a location. Thus:

constant PI = 3.14159

[†]The examples given from here on, unless specifically stated otherwise, do not necessarily correspond to any particular language and are used for purposes of illustration only.
[††]Some high-level languages permit mixed types of data in a single statement (mixed types being integer and floating point in this example). Other languages require consistency of type; these are called "strongly typed" languages.

is an instruction to the compiler to substitute the real number 3.14159 whenever it finds the label "PI" elsewhere in the program.

The compiler is aware of the distinction between the constant named "PI" and the variable named "B." When it sees the statement

C = B + PI

it will set up instructions to add the number 3.14159 to the contents of location B, storing the result in C; it will *not* attempt to generate code that uses the contents of location 3.14159 — even if such an address were possible!

A *literal* is almost the same as a constant, except that where the constant is used by the compiler to build part of the machine instruction, a literal is a fixed value stored in a memory location. It is thus like the variable, except that the program cannot change its contents. A very common use of this type of data is the text literal; for example, the compiler statement

string prompt = "Please answer Yes or No"†

will cause the compiler to set up the string of characters "Please answer Yes or No" (without the quotation marks) in memory, and assign the symbol "PROMPT" to be used as the address of the character string.

There is one other thing to note about the symbols "PI" and "PROMPT": they are meaningful names. Anyone reading a program which uses "PI" here and there will immediately know what the programmer's intention was. The same cannot be said for the symbols "A," "B," and "C" used in the earlier examples.

In the early years of high-level languages, it was not always

---

†Most languages will recognize instances of keywords and symbols without regard to case (C is a significant exception); but by convention, a string of characters inside quotation marks, as in this example, is stored as written and with no case conversion.

easy or convenient to come up with meaningful names. FOR-
TRAN in particular required an integer variable to be one whose
first letter was in the range I through N; variable names starting
with A through H and O through Z were used to hold real (floating point) numbers. Also, variable names were limited to six or
eight characters. Thus, while it was possible to use "PI" as a
meaningful symbol (fortunately, "P" is in the real number range),
an integer variable (or constant) could not be "COUNT_OF_
ITEMS" but would have to be "ICOUNT" or, more often, "I."
Once "I" was used, the next counter needed might be given the
name "II" or "J", and so on.

It so happens that there are occasionally valid uses for the
symbols "I" and "J", but the use of intrinsically meaningless labels such as "A" and "B" (or, for that matter, "FIRST" and "SEC-
OND") violates the principles of aesthetic programming. Such
violations have practical consequences: someone reading the program cannot easily grasp the purpose of the variables "A" and
"B", and so is more likely to misinterpret what the program is
doing. Even the programmer who wrote the code is likely to
forget their original intended usage, and reuse "A" and "B" for
some other purpose later in the program; that new usage might
interfere with the original—and still necessary—purpose of the
contents of A and B.

Almost all modern compilers will accept much longer symbols
these days, sometimes as many as 32 characters, which may be a
combination of letters, numbers, and other symbols such as "$" and
"_".[†] There is no excuse even for writing a line of code such as

ADD WAGE TO TOTAL

[†]The underscore is particularly useful for making a single name of out several words,
serving as it does in place of the space. Thus, THIS_WEEKS_WAGES is a single
variable name, while TOTAL WAGES would be two separate variables.

when

ADD THIS_WEEKS_WAGES TO TOTAL _WAGES

makes the intent of the operation much more clear.

Most modern languages, then, have essentially similar ways of establishing primitive or simple data structures — data that is composed of a single element. They may vary in the details of the wording, but basically they will use something along the lines of "long" or "integer" or "int" for an integer, "real" or "float" for a floating point number, and "char" or "byte" for a single character. Sometimes they will attach an adjective such as "signed" to make it clear that the integer is to be treated as a number and its sign (positive or negative), and "unsigned" for an absolute number. (Real numbers are always signed.) All of this information is needed for the compiler program to determine which machine instruction goes with the variable, constant, or literal being used.

Both high-level and assembly languages have means of organizing groups of these simple elements into arrays. An *array* is an ordered list of data elements all of the same size that for certain purposes we want to treat as a single unit. One of the simplest and most classic kinds of array is a *string*, a one-dimensional array of bytes or characters. Strings are so common that "string" has itself become a descriptor for them, as in the earlier example of the literal labelled "PROMPT." Similarly,

STRING Ask_for_number = "Enter a number from 1 to 999:"

defines an array whose name is "ASK_FOR_NUMBER" and whose (fixed) contents are the characters "E", "n", "t", "e", "r", " ", "a", etc., each character — including the space — occupying one byte. (Note that the spaces between the words are also characters and occupy one byte each.) An instruction such as

TYPE ASK_FOR_NUMBER

will cause the characters "Enter a number from 1 to 999:" to appear on the terminal screen when the program runs.

ASK_FOR_NUMBER and PROMPT are examples of a literal string, whose value does not change. A different type of a string is a variable, such as

STRING ANSWER[3]

which defines the memory location "ANSWER" to be three bytes long, but does not put anything in that space. (Square brackets are often used in data definitions to define the size of the array.) When the instruction

READ ANSWER

is executed, it will put the characters the user types in, into the three-byte field "ANSWER."

ANSWER is a small example of a *buffer*, a large space that is initially empty but that the program will fill as it proceeds. And both PROMPT and ANSWER are examples of a special class of one-dimensional arrays. Such arrays can be more generally defined by statements such as this one:

integer holidays[10]

which defines a set of ten integers (usually longwords) whose contents will be the Julian days (number of days of the year since January 1) that are legal holidays. The program will at some point set each element of the array to a value between 1 and 366. To look at a particular element in the array requires the use of an *index*, a variable or constant which describes the nth element of the array:

IF CURRENT_DAY = HOLIDAYS[J]

makes reference to the element "j" of the list of holidays ("J" being some other variable whose value has been previously set).[†]

Multidimensional arrays (matrices) are also possible:

integer holidays[100][10]

can hold all the holidays for a century, organized by year.

It is also possible to organize simple data types into a more complex *structure*, which will group together different types of data elements that are in some way related. This is one of those areas where languages are most likely to display individual idiosyncrasies, but let us imagine as an example a structure to contain information about a country:

structure COUNTRY = {
        string name [20],
        integer legal_holidays[15],
        float currency_conversion,
        signed integer time_zone }

This defines a data structure to be called "country"; it contains space for a country name (up to twenty characters), a list of up to fifteen legal holidays, a floating point (real) number which is

---

[†]One complication, that I will touch on only briefly, is that the elements of an array are numbered starting from zero or from one, depending on what the high-level language design will allow. Indeed, some languages allow arrays to start and end at any number. Writing a program using zero-based indexing when the array starts from one (or vice versa) is a common error.

the conversion factor to U.S. dollars, and the number of hours plus or minus Greenwich to calculate the local time. (Obviously, we are not dealing with Russia and its eleven time zones!) A program statement can make reference to an element of the structure:

TYPE COUNTRY.NAME

or to the structure as a whole: "COUNTRY," meaning the address of the start of the structure. Such a structure can itself be an array, so that if I define my structure as:

structure country[300] . . .

I can build a data structure for the whole United Nations. Referencing an individual item in such a structure can get interesting; to find the seventh holiday in country 150 requires an operand in the form

COUNTRY[150].LEGAL_HOLIDAYS[7]

That such an operand is all I need to get to that particular item demonstrates the power and flexibility of high-level languages. The actual machine instructions to calculate that location may be quite complex, but the burden of setting up those instructions has now been shifted to the compiler. It is an extension of how all these data forms lay out the contents of memory, so that the compiler knows which machine operations to select to properly describe these contents to the central processor. At the same time, the names that we give to each data element and structure help us to understand how the data is to be used.

12

CLASSES AND TYPES OF STATEMENTS

Data definitions such as the ones used in the previous chapter establish which type of machine instruction (character, integer, floating point, etc.) to use with each particular constant or variable, array or structure. Program statements are those that lay out the actual instructions of the program, and are the lines that the compiler translates into actual machine code.[†]

Every language, and every language manual, has its own methodology, terminology, and way of classifying the types of program statements that are included in the language. But for purposes of describing the overall concepts, we can divide these statements into three general classes: *operation*, *control*, and *function*.

[†]In an actual language, especially in the more sophisticated ones, data definitions will sometimes cause machine instructions to be generated, while some program statements operate at the compiler level only and do not generate any executable code. Still others (object definitions in particular) are a mix of the two. For a conceptual discussion, however, it is easier to see program statements and data definitions as conceptually distinct.

Operation statements are statements that actually do something, such as calculate a value, read a response from the terminal, or move data from place to place. The class of operation statements is divisible into two types: *data transport* and *data transformation*. Both types of operation statements take a similar form:

result = operand [operator [operand]] . . .

By this I mean that an operation statement specifies one or more *operands*, which means any of the data forms—variable, constant, literal, structure—discussed in the previous chapter. Some number of operations (or none) are performed on these operands, specified by the *operators* (plus sign, minus sign, etc.). Operands and their operators appear to the right of the equal sign, and the result is stored in the location specified on the left side of the equal sign.

The simplest form of an operation statement has one operand and zero operators:

A = 1

which means "store 1 in location A."

It is important to note that the equal sign does *not* mean "equality" in the mathematical sense. The statement above does not mean "A is equal to 1"; it means "assign the value 1 to location A." For this reason, this type of statement is often called an assignment statement.[†] A statement such as:

A = A + 1

[†]ALGOL 60 attempted to escape this confusion by using := instead of the equal sign; however, with the exception of PASCAL and ADA, this usage does not seem to have caught on (possibly because FORTRAN, which uses the equal sign, was already more popular).

is a mathematical absurdity, but it makes perfect sense in pro-gramming; what it means is: "Add 1 to A and store the result in A" — in other words, increment the value in A by 1.[†]

The next observation to be made about such a statement is that, because the equal sign is a symbol of assignment and not of equality, it is not possible to transpose the operands. That is, the statement

$$A + 1 = A$$

is invalid and will be marked as an error by any compiler. By long-standing convention, the element on the left side of the equal sign describes the location where the result of the operation is to be stored. Thus, it must be (for the most part) a single element name. And it must be a variable, not a constant; if, as in the previous chapter, PI was defined as a constant with the value 3.14159, it is absurd and invalid to attempt to write

$$PI = PI + 1$$

as an operation statement.[‡]

A third observation about the statement

$$A = 1$$

is that the compiler has already been given the definition of "A" (longword, floating point, etc.) and will therefore generate the

---

[†]Some languages allow a form of operation statements that combines the operand and the result in the same variable, and so avoid the equal sign altogether. In these languages, we might be able to write a statement such as "A++" as a shorthand way of saying "A = A + 1."

[‡]As noted in the previous chapter, the equal sign is often used in a data definition statement to establish the value of a constant. One must be careful not to confuse the different uses of this symbol.

appropriate instructions to store 1 at location A using the proper size and shape. Many (but not all) languages will also include instructions to convert from one size and shape to another, if the definitions of the variables are different. For example,

A = B

will generate a simple MOVE instruction (or the equivalent LOAD and STORE) if both A and B have been defined as the same data type (for example, LONG or BYTE). If A is a floating point variable, while B is an integer longword, some language compilers will when translating this into machine code include a CONVERT instruction. In other "strongly typed" languages, the compiler will mark this as an error, unless the programmer includes an explicit statement that conversion is to be performed.

Another point that needs to be borne in mind is that the value currently stored at the location on the left side of the equal sign is irrelevant—it will be overwritten by the assignment action. However, all the values on the right side of the equal sign must be known at the time the statement is executed. While the statement

A = 1

can be executed at any time because the value on the right side is a constant and thus known, the statements

A = B

and

A = A + 1

cannot execute properly unless the values of the variables—A and B—have been set earlier on in the course of the execution of the program.

Statements of the type

A = 1

and

A = B

are examples of what I call the *transport* type of statement: They transport the value of a variable from one location to another, or they transport a constant to a location. While in most cases transportation involves movement of scalar (single) values, in some languages it is possible to use a single assignment statement to transport all or part of one array or structure to another:

STRING1 = STRING2

or

STRING1 = STRING2 [1:10]

the latter example meaning copy ten characters of STRING2, starting at position 1, to STRING1. A variation on this is string concatenation:

NEW_STRING = STRING1 + STRING2

which copies STRING1 to NEW_STRING, followed immediately by STRING2.

String concatenation, though it looks like a transforming expression, does not change the contents of the strings but only moves them. Therefore, I have grouped it with the transport type, although it is a special case. In order to be classed as a *data transformation* statement, it must describe operations on the right side of the equal sign that change — *transform* — the data in some way.

Operands, as we have seen from the examples above, can be either constants (PI, 1) or variables (B). Operators come in various forms, depending on the language, but can be generally classed as arithmetic or logical in type, and unary or binary in form.

The simplest form of these is the *unary* operator: that is, an operator with one operand. The most common (sometimes the only) such operator is the minus sign:

$$A = -B$$

which means "store the negation of the value of B in A." Note that this does not necessarily mean that a negative value will be stored in A; if B contains -5, then the result in A will be $+5$.

A subtle variation on this statement form is one that appears to be a simple data transport statement:

$$A = B$$

where "A" is defined as an integer type, and "B" as a floating point number. The machine instructions that are compiled as a result of this statement will (depending on the machine, the language, and the compiler) either truncate the floating point, dropping everything to the right of the decimal point, or else round it off in some way. In either case, it performs a transformation on the data. This is one of the reasons why some languages are "strongly typed" and prohibit or limit this sort of action; it can lead to all kinds of errors if the conversion was unintended. Also, it may destroy the ability of the program to run on any other machine. At the very least, when using this sort of operation it is essential to include a comment explaining it.[†]

All other standard arithmetic operators are *binary*, which is to say they require two operands. All languages recognize the four basic arithmetic operators (some have special ones in addition to these):

+   addition
−   subtraction
*   multiplication
/   division

A simple arithmetic operation statement might be

PROFIT = PRICE − COST

which translates into the machine instructions to subtract the value in COST from the value in PRICE, storing the result in location PROFIT.

More complex operation statements are easily formed by combining operands and operators, but now an ambiguity arises: which operation is to be performed first in a statement such as this one?

X = A * −I + Y / Z − 150000

From the time of the first high-level languages, a variation on the standard mathematical conventions has been used to establish operator *precedence* for such situations. A few languages may have variations or additional operators, but all are agreed on this much, at least:

[†]And this is a simple example. In a language that permits implicit type conversion, any complex statement can have this sort of transformation buried in the middle of it.

1) Unary operators have precedence over binary.

2) Exponentiation (that is, "X squared" or "Y to the fourth power," often written as "X ** 2" or "Y ∧ 4") has precedence over all other binary operators.

3) Multiplication and division have equal precedence.

4) Addition and subtraction have equal precedence after multiplication and division.

5) Where two operators have equal precedence, operator evaluation proceeds from left to right.

6) An operation in parentheses has precedence over all others. If parentheses are nested, the innermost operation has precedence.[†]

Under these rules, the statement

$$X = A * -I + Y / Z - 150000$$

is executed thusly:

1) Take the negative of I.

2) Multiply the value in step 1 times A.

3) Divide Y by Z.

[†]Where implicit type conversion is allowed, it should take precedence over everything except a parenthetical expression.

4) Add the value from step 2 to the value in step 3.

5) Subtract 150,000 from the value in step 4.

6) Store the result in X.

Parentheses can effect a completely different set of execution steps. Rewriting the above statement as

$$X = A * (-(I + Y) / Z) - 150000$$

causes these steps to be performed:

1) Add I to Y.

2) Negate the value from step 1.

3) Divide the value from step 2 by Z.

4) Multiply A times the value from step 3.

5) Subtract 150,000 from the value in step 4.

6) Store the result in X.

Logical operation statements have the same form as arithmetic statements, but the operators are different and not quite as universal in definition. Logical operands, unlike arithmetic ones, have only two possible values: TRUE or FALSE.

Logical operators can also be unary or binary. The classic unary operator is "NOT":

$$A = NOT\ B$$

If B is FALSE, then A is set to TRUE; if B is TRUE, then the result stored in A is FALSE.[†]

Other logical operators are binary:

AND   If both operands are TRUE, then TRUE, else FALSE.

OR   If either operand is TRUE, then TRUE, else FALSE.

XOR   If one or the other operand is TRUE, then TRUE; if both operands are TRUE or both are FALSE, then FALSE.

While it is possible to combine arithmetic and logical expressions in the same operation statement, this can be tricky and sometimes leads to confusion on both the part of the programmer and of someone reading the program later on — and may result in different results depending on the language and its specific implementation. There is, however, one very common set of logical operations that is performed on arithmetic variables: *comparisons*.

Comparison operators are for the most part standardized:

=   If operands are equal, then TRUE, else FALSE.[‡]

>   If the first operand is greater than the second, then TRUE, else FALSE.

<   If the first operand is less than the second, then TRUE, else FALSE.

[†]The actual definition of TRUE and FALSE varies with the language and sometimes with the implementation of the language on a specific type of computer. In many cases, zero is used to mean FALSE and any nonzero value is taken as TRUE, but this should not be taken for granted; refer to the description of the specific language — and be especially careful when mixing two languages!

[‡]Unfortunately, this is yet another use of the same equal sign, this time testing for equality, and not establishing it. It is usually clear from context. Some languages use other symbols to avoid confusion; thus, in C, $==$ is used to test for equality.

For example, the expression

COST < PRICE

yields the value TRUE if the value in COST is less than the value in PRICE, and FALSE if COST is greater than or equal to PRICE.

Often times these symbols are combined, so that NOT= (or !=) results in TRUE if the operands are different, while >= yields TRUE if the first operand is greater than or equal to the second. Thus, the expression

PRICE >= COST

produces a slightly different result from the previous expression: it is TRUE if PRICE is greater than or equal to COST (that is, COST is less than or equal to PRICE), and false otherwise. The difference is that in the first expression, the resulting value is FALSE if the two variables are equal, while in the second expression, when the variables are equal the result is TRUE.[†]

It is possible to use these comparison expressions in an operation statement, storing a TRUE or FALSE result in a location, but by far the greatest use of these operators is in *control statements*.

Normally, a program executes operation statements in sequence, one following the other in the computer much as it does on the page—from top to bottom, beginning to end. However, when it becomes necessary to alter the flow of execution, the programmer must use some type of control statement rather than an operation.

The class of control statements may be divided conceptually

[†]As this example shows, comparison operations can be extremely tricky and a major source of program errors.

into three types: *alternative, iterative,* and *directive.* The first type selects an operation from two (or more) alternatives; the second repeats an operation some number of times; and the third unconditionally redirects the computer to some other location in the program.

The classic alternative control statement is the *if*—if some condition is TRUE, then perform the following statement; if not, skip it. For example:

    if COST < PRICE
        then profit = price − cost

When the program executes, machine instructions will compare the contents of COST to the contents of PRICE. If COST is less than PRICE, then the computer will perform the operation statement to calculate PROFIT; otherwise it will skip that statement and go on to the next one.

Another form of this statement offers two alternatives; instead of "do this or not," we can instruct the computer to "do this or else do that":

    if COST < PRICE
        then profit = price − cost
        else loss = cost − price

If it costs less to produce an item than the price it is being sold for, then the difference between the two is the profit. Otherwise ("else") the difference is the loss. This type of control statement is by far the most common of the alternatives, and is usually referred to as an *if-then-else* statement.

In some languages, a less common alternative statement exists that instructs the computer to choose from among several statements at once, based on the contents of some variable.

Known as the *switch* or *case* statement, it has the general form:[†]

switch (expression):
        [alternative 1]: statement
        [alternative 2]: statement . . .
        [alternative n]: statement
        [otherwise]: statement

In this type of statement, the computer evaluates the switch expression (which is usually a variable, but may be an expression or even a function call) and selects from among the alternate statements the one whose value ("alternative 1", "alternative 2", etc.) matches the value of the expression. If none of them match, then the "otherwise" statement (if any) is executed. As may be seen from this explanation, *switch* is the equivalent of a special combination of *if-then-else* statements, which presented in this way avoids the confusion that may result from trying to follow a collection of *if* after *if* after *if*.

The iterative type of control statement performs an operation over and over again until some condition is satisfied. The basic type of iterative control statement is the *loop*, generally in the form of a *do-while:*

DO operation WHILE condition

That is, perform this operation as long as the stated condition is true. Thus, if A currently contains the value 1, then:

DO A = A + 1 WHILE A < 10

[†]Switch statements are not standardized, and the exact syntax will differ for each language that has this type of alternative statement.

will execute nine times, while the value of A changes from 2 to 10.

The condition can precede the expression:

WHILE A < 10 DO A = A + 1

The difference between the two forms is that in the latter the condition is tested *before* each iteration. In the first statement, the expression "A = A + 1" will be executed at least once, no matter what value A contains at the start, while in the second statement if A is greater than or equal to 10 at the start, the expression is never executed at all. Each of the two modes of operation has its uses, and a programmer must be aware of the difference.

A programmer must also be aware of the possibilities for infinite looping that *do-while* constructions can create. A simple example of an *infinite loop* would be:

WHILE A < 10 DO B = B + 1

The expression "B = B + 1" does not change the condition in any way. Depending on the value of A at the time the loop is encountered, the loop will either not execute at all or will execute forever.

Incrementing a value, particularly an index to an array, is so common that a special form of iterative control statement is often used: the *for* loop. In this type of statement, a variable is given an initial value, a transformation statement (generally "increment by 1"), and a final value or condition. For example, to initialize all the elements in an array of 10 elements to zero, we might use a statement such as:

FOR i = 1 TO 10 BY 1
    array[i] = 0

which sets the variable i to 1 as its initial value, performs the associated operation, then increments i ("BY 1").[†] And for as long as i is less than or equal to 10, it will repeat this process.

Alternative or iterative control statements can be combined to many levels; this is called *nesting*—one loop nests inside the other. Thus, to initialize a two-dimensional array that is 10 × 100 elements, one might write:

```
FOR i = 1 TO 10 BY 1
    FOR j = 1 TO 100 BY 1
        matrix[i,j] = 0
```

in which the inner "j" loop executes 100 times for every "i" iteration, and the "i" loop executes ten times.

Although the examples shown are relatively simple, it is not hard to imagine nestings within nestings that are difficult to follow. Using a *for* loop can also lead to inefficiencies; if a program has a loop that searches an array until it matches some value, there ought to be a way to escape from the loop once the value is found.

This leads to the third type of control statement: the *directive*. Unlike the other types, a directive control statement unconditionally alters the flow of the program by directing it to go elsewhere. One such directive, *break*, is often used to "break out" of a nested loop to the next level or beyond.[‡] The *continue* statement is similar to the *break*, except that it merely breaks out of the current iteration and "continues" with the next one. Another

---

[†]Recall from the previous chapter that the phrase "array[i]" means the ith element of *array*—in other words, *i* is an index into *array*. This statement demonstrates a classic method of accessing all of the elements of an array one element at a time.
[‡]*Break* can also be used in a *switch*-type construction to prevent the execution of a statement one alternative from continuing on to the next one.

very useful directive is the *return* statement, which lets a function know when it has finished. The return statement will be discussed in Chapter 13.

The most famous — and most reviled — form of directive is the *goto*. As its name implies, it directs the computer to "go to" some other location in the program. In languages such as FORTRAN and COBOL, this location can be anywhere in the program: in some distant routine in a far-off module; in the middle of a "for" loop whose iteration counter now becomes meaningless; even (in the case of assembly language) into the middle of data space. Jumping into the middle of data generally causes an immediate fatal reaction; jumping into some unintended location in the program may allow it to continue for a while, but with unpredictable results. As a consequence, structured programming purists have argued for the elimination of *goto* or at least for severe restrictions on its use. Many language textbooks discourage its use; others, such as some of the ones written for the JAVA language, do not even like to talk about it.[†]

Goto, however, is not without its advantages. Used sparingly and within a limited range, it can be useful for breaking out of convoluted situations such as deeply nested loops — and thus avoids the ambiguity that *break* can cause by showing exactly how many levels of nesting are being abandoned. And some languages do not have any other means of escaping a section of code. A FORTRAN example shows how *goto* might be used when searching a two-dimensional array for a particular match:

[†]One JAVA textbook lists *goto* as a reserved but unused keyword (Author and Makower 1996, 131). Another calls the *goto* statement "evil" (Niemeyer and Peck 1996, 60). On the other hand, Holub (1995, 92–94) finds some limited uses for *goto* in C.

```
          DO 10 I = 1, 100
          DO 10 J = 1, 100
10        IF (ARRAY (I,J) .EQ. MATCH) GO TO 50
20 . . .
```

This nested loop searches the 100×100 ARRAY for the first entry that equals the contents of MATCH. If it finds one, it goes to the instruction at 50; if it goes through all entries without finding a match, it continues execution at 20.

The following rules will, if carefully observed, exploit the potentialities of *goto* without exposing the program to its dangers:

1) A *goto* statement is used only to escape from the interior of a nested loop or nested set of tests when it is clear that there is no point in continuing further with that section of code. It can also be used to direct the program to an exit routine when the situation has deteriorated to the point of catastrophe and an execution abort is required.[†]

2) The *goto* and the program location that it goes to (defined by a *label*) are close to each other, no more than one page apart, except in the case of an abort routine.

3) The label is a meaningful symbol; that is, the label describes the action — "abort_input:", for example.

4) The label is placed at the start of an operation statement or control sequence; it is never placed in the middle of a loop or *if-then-else* construction.

[†]For example, in a section of code that reads in data from a file, there might be a line such as "IF (read_error) THEN GOTO abort_input".

5) A *goto* always goes in a forward direction, never back to code already executed.

6) Each *goto* uses a separate label; no two *goto* statements go to the same location.

The point of these guidelines is that it should be immediately clear to anyone reading the code just where it is going—and equally to the point, when one reaches its destination, it should be obvious and unambiguous where it came from. The programmer maintains control over the program by being aware at any given point in the program how to get there, what to do there, and where to go next.

Operation statements, alternative and iterative control statements, and directive statements all have a certain amount of power on their own. But it is when they are combined in groups that they really begin to reveal their potential.

Up to this point the control statements I have described cause the execution of, at most, a single operation statement. (See the aforementioned *if-then-else* statement that decides whether to charge a profit or a loss for an example.) Most programming tasks, however, require multiple operations to be performed while some condition applies. In order to avoid any ambiguity in determining where the condition ends, languages require that such a set of statements be organized into a *block* of code.

A block is delimited by special keywords or symbols, most commonly *begin-end* or "{" and "}," known as the "squiggly brackets." All the statements within the block are executed when the alternative control statement is TRUE for them, or for as long as an iterative control statement is TRUE for them. Thus, a fragment of code to determine how much profit was made from today's sales might look something like this:

```
todays_profit = 0
profit_sales = 0
BEGIN
    INTEGER new_sale
    READ (new_sale)
    WHILE (new_sale > 0) DO
    BEGIN
       IF cost [new_sale] < price[new_sale]
          THEN
             BEGIN
                todays_profit = todays_profit +
                        (price[new_sale] − cost[new_sale])
                profit_sales = profit_sales + 1
             END
          ELSE
             BEGIN
                todays_profit = todays_profit −
                   (cost[new_sale] − price [new_sale])
             END
          READ (new_sale)
    END
END.†
```

This simple code (again, a number of statements have been omitted for clarity) begins with the initialization of a couple of variables by reading in the first sale from some file or other col-

---

†In most languages, with the significant exception of C (and now JAVA as well), whether a word is in upper- or lowercase is irrelevant. I have put keywords in uppercase and symbols in lowercase for ease of reading.

lection. It loops through all the day's sales, each time getting a new value for the variable "new_sale" until it reaches the last sale ("new_sale" has a value of zero). For each sale where the cost of the item is less than it was sold for, the difference is added to the day's total profit, and the number of profitable sales is increased by one. Where the cost was greater, the difference is subtracted.

There is no intrinsic limit to the number of statements within a *begin-end* block, nor to the number of such blocks nested within one another. There does come a point when it is difficult for the eye to distinguish among the blocks and the code contained therein. One remedy is to indent the inner blocks as shown above; these indentations mean nothing to a compiler, but they mean a great deal to the human reader. Other techniques involve substituting functions for blocks of code, which we will come to shortly.

But first, there is another use for dividing code into blocks besides demarcating a set of code. Even more important, blocks delineate the *scope* of a variable name; that is, they specify the section of code wherein a variable name is meaningful.

The concept of scope is that it restricts the use of a variable name to a specific section of code, and thus limits the number of instructions that have access to the location defined by that variable name. In the simple code example above, the integer variable "new_sale" is defined *inside* the *begin-end* block, and so only those instructions within this block can examine or modify this string. The variables *todays_profit*, *profit_sales*, and so on are not defined within this block, so we know that their scope is wider than just this piece of code.

Limiting access to a particular location is crucial to ensuring that the location contains the data it is intended to have. In the ultimate program that is machine language, as well as in its assembly language cognates, instructions have few restrictions on the data they can read and modify. But this freedom comes with a price: if the contents of a location are unexpectedly altered, it can be difficult to determine just where the alteration occurred — in the section of code that was intended to work with this location, or in an unrelated section fifteen pages away. And if it is difficult enough for a single programmer to keep track of all the variables in use in a small program, this difficulty increases exponentially when the program is the product of a team of five, ten, or fifty programmers.

Modern language compilers allow a programmer to specify that a particular variable name has meaning only within a limited scope — that is, within the block of code designated by *begin* and *end*. The variable defined at the start of the block has meaning only to the code contained within the block, and not elsewhere. Thus it becomes possible to use variables with standard meanings, such as i and j, for example (the most commonly used names for indices), in different parts of the program without fear of ambiguity or conflict.

The organization of code into these block structures is one of the major elements in structured programming, and it is extremely useful in letting the programmer control which parts of the program will manipulate which elements of data. A program is no longer a large undifferentiated sequence of statements, but a clearly structured set of code blocks, each of which has a single task to perform. Each block has its own set of local variables and instructions — operations, control statements, and function calls — through which it does its job. The block structure is so basic that it is used to construct the ultimate program itself — the procedure or function.

13

THE FUNCTIONAL PROGRAM

Those who wrote the first computer programs quickly discovered that it did not pay to reinvent the wheel each time. If someone had already written and tested a block of code to calculate a square root, it was easier to ask for a copy of the procedure than to work it out all over again. Informal code-sharing soon developed into formal libraries of reliable routines, and by 1951, David Wheeler of the Cambridge group had worked out an efficient mechanism for loading such routines anywhere in memory so that another program could use them (Campbell-Kelly and Aspray 1996, 186). These blocks of code became known as *subroutines* (that is, subordinate to the main routine or program).

In order to use a subroutine, the main program issues a machine instruction known as a *call* (or a similar instruction, such as "jump to subroutine"), which changes the execution flow to the start of the subroutine while at the same preserving the address of the next instruction in the main program: the "return address." The last instruction in the subroutine code is a *return* instruction, which again changes the execution flow—this time back to the instruction at the return address. Because the return address is saved in this fashion, the main program can call the subroutine from many different places, and each time when the subroutine is finished the main program will continue from where it left off.

In the earliest computers, the return address was saved in a special register. This quickly became a serious limitation, however, for it meant that one subroutine could not call another; if it did, it would replace the first subroutine's return address with the one for the second subroutine, and the program would get totally lost. To solve this problem, hardware engineers came up with the concept of a *stack*.

A stack consists of an area of memory and a pointer to some location within that area. Whenever a *call* instruction executes, it "pushes" the return address onto the stack by incrementing the stack pointer to the next location in the memory stack and then storing the return address in that location. When the subroutine executes the *return* instruction, this "pops" the return address from the location that the stack pointer describes and then adjusts the stack pointer to the previous location.[†] This stack is analogous to a pile of dishes, where the last dish placed on top of the pile is the first one to be removed. Such a stack makes it possible for one subroutine to call another, and so on and so on, up to the limit of the stack capacity.

For example, say we have a subroutine, SUBR1, that needs

[†]Different computers will vary in the details of stack manipulation, but the principle is the same for all of them. Most of them will also have circuitry that checks for stack overflow and underflow (pushing on too much and popping off too much).

some action which a second subroutine, SUBR2, can perform. Because stack management eliminates the need to worry about storing the return addresses correctly, the subroutines can be written as

```
SUBR1:
    BEGIN
        :
        :
        CALL SUBR2
        :
        RETURN
    END
SUBR2:
    BEGIN
        :
        RETURN
    END
```

When, in the main program, the computer executes the instruction

```
CALL SUBR1
```

it will preserve the address of the following instruction on the stack and proceed to execute the code at SUBR1. In the middle of that code is the call to SUBR2. The computer preserves the following address on the stack on top of the first address it saved earlier, and proceeds to execute SUBR2. When SUBR2 is done, and the computer executes the RETURN statement, it takes the most recent address it put on the stack—the location in SUBR1—and continues execution from there. The RETURN statement at the end of SUBR1 performs a similar function, this time returning control to the location in the main program just after the original CALL instruction.

The stack also makes it easier to pass parameters to the subroutine. A *parameter* is some data that the subroutine needs to fulfill its function. In the case of the square root subroutine, the subroutine needs to know the number of which it is supposed to take the square root; this is its parameter.

Prior to the creation of stacks, parameters had to be passed by placing them in some previously arranged location; this made them tricky to work with and gave rise to the chance that two subroutines might inadvertently use the same location. But just as an address can be pushed onto a stack, so too can the parameters. Now, in order to call a subroutine, the programmer only has to know the order of the parameters and their type. The program pushes them onto the stack in order and then calls the subroutine. The subroutine removes them from the stack in reverse order and operates on them, finally using the return address when it is done.[†]

Parameters can be divided into two basic types: *call-by-value* and *call-by-reference* (along with a few others that are obscure and rarely used). A call-by-value parameter pushes onto the stack the actual data that is to be used; if we need to find the square root of 25, we will pass the actual number "25" to the subroutine. In other cases, however, we need to pass more data than can be held in a single stack location. For example, we may call a TYPE subroutine to display "My name is HAL" on the terminal screen. The string of characters "My name is HAL" is too long to fit easily on the stack, so instead we push the *address* of the string

[†]In order to avoid complicated juggling and potential confusion between the parameters and the return address, many computers now use a separate stack for each. But the principle is the same: push down and pop up.

onto the stack—which makes it a call-by-reference. Any combination of call-by-value and call-by-reference parameters may precede the actual subroutine call.

A subroutine also generally has a *return value*: In the case of the square root subroutine, the return value is the calculated square root. By convention, the return value is passed back to the calling program in a particular register. But a general purpose register holds only a limited amount of data, generally one longword. When a subroutine has more data to pass back, the calling program must pass it the address of some *buffer* as a call-by-reference; the subroutine fills up the buffer and returns to the caller when done. For example, in order to use a READ subroutine, the program pushes down the address of a buffer large enough to contain the input text, and the READ subroutine will store the input characters there.

The return value is often used in combination with a return buffer; in the case of the READ subroutine, the return value can be used to indicate how many characters were read in. (And if the return value is zero or negative, this will be understood to mean that the read operation failed.) It should be clear by now that while the computer hardware facilitates the use of subroutines, much of the way we use them is established by convention. Any subroutine library is accompanied by documentation describing which parameters to pass and in what order, where the output from the subroutine is placed and in what format, and what the return value (if used) signifies.

Libraries, or files containing a collection of subroutines, are especially useful to programmers. They constitute perhaps the primary tool that enables us to avoid the process of solving the same problem all over again—including making many of the same mistakes. A library subroutine is expected to be thoroughly tested and proved; it frees us from worrying about at least that particular coding task. A computer vendor will usually ship some standard system libraries with the operating system, and software houses often offer specialized libraries for sale, containing, for example, complex mathematical and scientific calculation routines, or database manipulation programs.

We are now prepared to discuss how high-level languages make subroutine calls, and how these calls are the backbone of structured programming. Structured programming is so dependent on this calling structure that it has expanded its use far beyond what the term "subroutine" might imply. A better term for this expanded functionality, then, is *function*, which conveys the idea that the routine being called performs some function that may be as small as the traditional subroutine or so large as to encompass the entire program.

In mathematics the classic use of a function is in the form

$$y = f(x)$$

where "f" is some function, "x" is the variable on which it operates, and "y" is the result. In most computer languages (COBOL being a major exception), a *function call* takes a similar form:

$$Y = SQRT (X)$$

This program statement calls the square root subroutine (function), passing it the value of X as a parameter, and placing the result (the return value) in Y.

In the previous chapter I discussed operation statements, control statements, and operands. The function call encompasses all three concepts. It is a control statement in that it causes the execution flow of the program to change, even if only temp-orarily. It is an operation statement in that it performs operations that transform and transport data. And it is an operand in that it is an element on the right side of an assignment statement.

Because it is an operand (and because the stack mechanism makes nested function calls possible), a function call can also be a parameter to another function call:

Y = SIN (SQRT (X))

passes the value of X to the square root function, passes the result of the square root to the SIN function, and stores the return value from the SIN function in Y. (Recall the rules of precedence in the previous chapter; operations inside the parentheses always have precedence over all other operations.)[†]

How the compiler knows whether the parameters are passed by value or by reference is determined in part by a program statement that describes the function and its *formal parameters*. Details vary from language to language, but in essence this is a formal statement that does not actually generate any machine code but defines for the compiler the nature of the parameters that the function will need when it is actually called further down in the program. A formal statement may look something like:

int MY_FUNCTION (int A, char @B, signed byte C)

This statement describes a function with three parameters: A, B, and C. The first parameter is an integer (longword) passed as call

†Not only can function calls be nested, a function can even call itself—a process known as *recursion*. While recursion can be extremely useful in solving problems with an indeterminate number of steps, it can also be dangerous: If the function does not know when to stop calling itself, it will get into a state of "infinite recursion," stopping only when it runs out of stack space.

by value. The second parameter is a character string that is passed by reference (the at-sign means "address of"), while the third parameter, again passed by value, is a signed byte. The return value of the function is an integer as well; we need to define the data type of the return value just as we would for any variable. The compiler cannot accept the use of a function call as an operand unless it knows its data type and thus what machine instructions to use with it.

In some languages, a program must include a formal statement of each function it intends to use, whether the function is defined later in the program or is located in a separate library. The compiler matches the formal parameter list against the list used in the actual function call, and marks the call as being in error if the two lists do not match. There are some compilers that operate without a formal list, and determine call-by-value or call-by-reference setup based on the data type of the actual parameter. When this is allowed, the programmer must be even more careful to get the parameters right; otherwise, the error may not be uncovered until testing and sometimes not until the program has gone into production. Other languages make the programmer spell out the nature of each parameter as part of the function. A call to MY_FUNCTION in COBOL, for example, would have to say:

```
CALL "my_function" USING BY VALUE a BY REFERENCE b
        BY VALUE c GIVING return_code.
```

Sometimes there is no need for a function to supply a return value. For example, suppose we want to the program to suspend itself for a specific period of time while other activity is taking place. A function call such as

```
SLEEP (15)
```

would suspend the program for fifteen seconds. When the program is reawakened, there is nothing that the return value could tell us—we already know we are awake again. This is an instance of a function call used purely as a statement and not as an operand.

In other cases we may not even have any parameters to pass to the function. To ring the bell or buzzer on a terminal, for example, we need only use the function call

RING_BELL ()

and the bell will ring. This example also serves to illustrate a secondary aspect of the function call: the parentheses are used not just for the purpose of defining the parameters to be passed, but also to alert the compiler that RING_BELL is a function call rather than a data element.

Just because a function needs no parameters does not mean it does not have a return value. A function call to determine the number of seconds the program has been running might be called as

SECONDS_UP = GET_RUNTIME ()

This function needs no parameters; it simply passes back the integer number of seconds of CPU time that the program has so far accumulated. As these illustrations show, there is a wide variety of combinations which can be applied to a function call.

What these illustrations also show is that requests to the operating system for various actions and information—to suspend the program, to get the CPU runtime—also take the form of function calls. The actual machine instructions may be slightly different than a *call* op code, but the concept is the same. This is deliberately done so that a programmer can use the same structure for internal subroutines, library routines, and system services, and combine them all into program statements. Suppose a programmer has written a subroutine that takes an integer in binary form and converts it into a decimal string of characters (for instance, 11010001, whose decimal value is 209, is converted to the character string "2", "0", and "9"). The return value of this function is the address of the character string. The program statement

TYPE (CONVERT_TO_DECIMAL (GET_RUNTIME ()))[†]

calls the system service GET_RUNTIME to get the number of CPU seconds (in binary); the return value (output) is then passed as a parameter to the programmer's own CONVERT_TO_DECIMAL code. The output from that function is the address of a character (text) buffer, which is given to the TYPE system service to display on the screen.

Whether a system service, library subroutine, or user-written local function, the body of the function consists of any number of operation and control statements — and possibly other function calls — and at least one *return* statement at the point where the function is done. In high-level languages, *return* may be followed by a value (constant or variable) in parentheses; this is the language syntax that describes what the return value will be. The function body also may contain definitions for data elements that it needs locally but which the rest of the program does not need

---

[†]Yes, all the parentheses are necessary — and it is easy to lose count of them! Mismatched parentheses are among the most common syntax errors.

to know about. In order to accomplish all this, we define a function body by using the block structure technique described at the end of the previous chapter.

A simple function to determine which of two alphabetic characters come first in sequence (regardless of whether they are in upper- or lowercase) might look like this:

```
logical IN_SEQUENCE (char first, char second)
BEGIN
     char temp_first, temp_second
          temp_first = convert_to_upper (first)
          temp_second = convert_to_upper (second)
          IF temp_first <= temp_second
               THEN RETURN (TRUE)
               ELSE RETURN (FALSE)
END
```

This function definition begins with a formal statement that identifies its name and describes it as having two formal parameters, FIRST and SECOND, each of which is an alphabetic character. (In a real program, the function would include a check to validate that the parameters were truly alphabetic.) The return value of the function is defined as logical, meaning it will be one of the two logical values: TRUE or FALSE.

The next line of the function defines two local character values, TEMP_FIRST and TEMP _SECOND. Because these values are defined within the function block (BEGIN-END), they cannot be used by any code outside the block—which is just as well, since they are meaningless anywhere else.

The function operation—what will become the executable code—consists of two calls to another function that has an alphabetic character as its parameter. If the character is uppercase, the return value is the character itself; otherwise CONVERT _TO _UPPER converts the lowercase character to uppercase and returns that as the value. Our function stores each of the return values in its local data space. Finally, the function compares the two characters and returns with a logical constant as its return value: TRUE if the first character is less than the second (as "A" is less than "B", for example) or the two characters are the same; FALSE if the first character is greater than the second.

A sorting program might use this function to determine the order of two characters:

```
IF IN_SEQUENCE (INPUT_1, INPUT_2)
     THEN
                 [put INPUT_1 first in sort order]
     ELSE
                 [put INPUT_2 first in sort order]
```

and so on.

While it is possible for the sort program to do the comparison in the body of the code rather than calling a function to do so, there are several reasons for doing it this way. In the first place, if the program needs to do the same comparison elsewhere, it would have to repeat the same code over again, which is wasteful duplication. Also, by writing and testing out the comparison function once, the programmer can be assured that the code is working; making a new call to a working subroutine is far less likely to introduce a new error than is typing the same code over again. Organizing the code into a block-structured function also ensures that any local variables it uses cannot be touched by any other program; it also ensures that the function will not accidently use some data it was not intended to see. The input to this piece of code, the internal manipulations of data, and the output from the code section are clearly defined and precisely controlled. Finally, and perhaps even most importantly, using functions in this way makes it easier to understand what the program is supposed to do.

This principle of breaking up the actual work of the program into smaller and smaller pieces, each described in a function structure, is at the heart of structured programming. In a structured environment, everything is a function, from the smallest detail of operation to the main program itself. A structured design session begins by breaking up the problem to be solved into smaller pieces; each piece is itself then broken up into smaller pieces, and so on, until each individual piece is small enough that its functionality can be clearly perceived. (Knowing when this stage has been reached is, even today, largely a matter of art, intuition, and programming style.) Often the individual pieces, or the basic functions, can be used by many different parts of the larger program. Breaking the program up into functions this way also makes it easy to assign different parts of the program to different programmers. The block structure of the function protects each programmer from interference by the others; my use of the variable name TEMP_FIRST in one function does not prevent another programmer three cubicles away from using the same variable name for a completely different function, since the variable is strictly local to my own code.

Another advantage of this approach is that each function can be tested separately and proven to work. This makes the job of combining the individual functions into larger and larger blocks of code much easier, since the major testing effort now focuses on making sure that the parameters and return values are used correctly rather than on worrying about the internal details of someone else's routine. Once I have coded and tested

IN_SEQUENCE, for example, and satisfied myself that it does exactly what it is supposed to, I — and others — can use it over and over again without any concern that it will cause problems. And if a problem does arise, the proper use of the function structure makes it easier and faster to isolate the part of the program where the problem is occurring.

A program constructed in this way consists of a series of function calls to other parts of the program, and they in turn consist of other calls and operations, and so on. A number of these functions may be grouped together into a single file of source code for convenience because they perform similar tasks, or even simply because they were written at the same time by the same programmer (which is not the best reason, but it happens a lot). Each such source file is often called a *module*; like many terms in this business, it has different meanings depending on who uses it. Generally, a module is a collection of program statements organized into a single source file and that, when given to a compiler, contains all the statements needed for that compiler to produce valid machine code as its output. This output is called an *object* file. A large program will consist of many modules (hundreds or even thousands in some cases), each of which will make reference to functions, system services, or library routines that are not defined within that module itself. The object files must therefore be combined somehow before there can be a working program that the computer can properly execute.

Combining these objects into a working program is the job of a program called the *linker*. This program accepts a list of object files and "links" them together so that a function call in one module is properly connected to the actual function code in another module. It also accesses the library files to get any functions it needs, and completes the setting up of the operating system service calls. The output from the linker is a single file called the "executable" or "runtime" program. It is this file that is finally loaded in memory for the computer to execute.

It should be understood that the link step is not limited to structured programs. Nor is it restricted to linking modules written in the same language; in fact, it is sometimes convenient to write some particular function in assembler language, or to use a mixture of high-level languages (though this can easily lead to complications if the programmer is not careful). The linker also performs other tasks related to the layout of memory, to the actual assignment of addresses of data space, and so on. Its primary goal, however, is establishing the final connections among the disparate function calls from the various pieces that together make up a functioning program.

Because the running program is itself a function—the operating system begins execution of the program by, in effect, issuing a *call* op code—it can, under some circumstances, be used in its entirety as a subordinate function to yet another program. In this fashion programmers build on previous work to craft new solutions to ever more complex problems. The modularity of structured programming goes a long way toward making this incredibly complex accumulation of code a working reality.

14

A SHORT COMMENTARY

Ultimately, binary is the only language the computer understands. All other computer languages — even assembly language — are poised at the boundary between human and machine and are in some form an attempt to improve communications between them. But the languages through which we instruct the computer are, in all cases, highly circumscribed. We do not use the same language or the same forms of language in programming that we use when speaking to another person. Computer languages are compact, they have rigid formulations and precise syntax, and the very structures which make them comprehensible to a computer also make them obscure to a human being.

From a programmer's perspective, then, the single most important type of statement in a computer language is the *comment*. A comment is text embedded in the source code which is marked in such a way that it will be ignored by the compiler. In FOR-

TRAN, a "C" in the leftmost position (a holdover from the days of punched cards) means this is a comment line; in COBOL, an asterisk in this same column does the job. In C and JAVA, anything between /* and */ is a comment, and this may be any text from a few words on the same line as the code to a whole paragraph or page. Assembly languages sometimes use a semicolon; from that character up to the end of the line is all text that the assembler will ignore.

But while it is of no concern to the compiler or assembler, the comment is crucial to the programmer. The comment is the part of the program that communicates not to the machine but to human beings, both the ones who wrote the code and the ones who will follow after. It must at all times be borne in mind that the source code that makes up a program is written as much for living people as it is for the machine. We are the ones who give the machine its instructions, and we are the ones who must take responsibility for our commands; therefore, we must be absolutely clear about what it is we are saying.

One might think that professional programmers, being fluent in the languages and techniques, need less explanation than an amateur or beginner, but this is not the case. Every programmer has certain idiosyncratic ways of doing things, and assumptions and methods that seem "obvious" at the time the code was written are very often unclear to another programmer on the same team, or even to the original programmer a few months later, when the code must be revisited for correction or modification. Every programming task also has hidden quirks and requirements; again, these may be obvious at the time, but who will remember all the details once the initial work is done and it is time to move on to another phase?

In the early days of programming, comments were often few

and far between. There was simply too much work to be done too fast, the code was changing constantly, and any comment written one day might become obsolete the next day and need to be rewritten. It meant typing up yet another punched card or taking up scarce disk space as well.

In addition, there was, and still is, a prevalent myth that code could be made self-documenting: If it were only written just so, the code would explain itself and would need no text intended for human eyes only. COBOL in particular is responsible for perpetuating this myth; one of the goals of the CODASYL committee was to create a computer language sufficiently close to English that nonprogrammers would feel comfortable reading a COBOL program, confident that they could understand what it was doing.[†] All that this intention accomplished, however, was to make COBOL that much more verbose. The statements of a COBOL program barely manage to cover *what* detailed actions the program takes; they give no insight into the overall functionality, nor can they explain *why* a particular step was done.

A comment serves primarily to answer the question "why" — what the programmer's intention was in using this instruction in this particular place. Without such an explanation, it is that much more difficult to analyze a piece of code that is causing trouble and to figure out whether the instruction really belongs there, what concern it was supposed to address, and whether changing or removing it will cause more problems than it solves.

Comments are also needed as part of the definition of a function or module. These comments describe what the function

---

[†]Even writing comments in COBOL can be awkward, as they cannot be placed on the same line as code, but must be on a separate line of their own. COBOL's Englishlike appearance also makes it harder for the reader to separate the comments from the code.

does, what its input requirements are, what values it returns and what side effects it causes. It has also become standard practice for each module to have a set of comments at the beginning listing the history of changes: who made them, when, and why.

All of this might seem to be so obvious a requirement as to be not worth mentioning, but I have spent much of a long career in computers wrestling with programs whose lack of comments left me with no idea of what they were supposed to do and what changes had been made to them. I have found myself staring at a piece of uncommented code at two in the morning, *knowing* that it was the cause of the present emergency, but having no idea what it was doing there, nor whether removing it might make things worse. At such an hour it is difficult to think charitably of the programmers who originally wrote that code, however rushed they may have been at the time.

Comments preserve a program's history and protect its destiny, and they help bridge the gap between us and our machines.

15

ALGORITHMS AND OBJECTS

An *algorithm* is a formula for solving a problem. Knuth quotes mathematical historians as tracing the origin of the word back to medieval Arabic, when the Persian mathematician al-Khowârizmi wrote *Kitab al jabr w'al-muqbala* ("Rules of restoration and reduction") around the year 825 CE. *Khowârizm* (the name of the city where the mathematician came from, today known as Khiva, in Uzbekistan), gradually mutated into *algorism*, and by 1747 had become *algorithmus* in Latin and was used by Leibniz, one of the inventors of calculus, to mean "ways of calculation" (Knuth 1973, 1–2).

The term as we use it today means a set of ordered steps that leads to a specified solution. For example, an algorithm to determine whether a particular year is a leap year would be:

1) If the year is not divisible by 4, then it is not a leap year.

2) If it is divisible by 4 and not a century year, then it is a leap year.

3) If it is a century, and divisible by 400, then it is a leap year, otherwise it is not.

The task of a computer programmer is to convert this algorithm into a language the computer can understand:

```
if year mod†/4 = 0           /* Is the year divisible by 4? */
  then                       /* It is. Then . . . */
    if year mod 100 not = 0  /* If it is not a century */
    or year mod 400 = 0      /* or it's divisible by 400 */
      then return TRUE       /* It's a leap year */
      else return FALSE      /* It's not a leap year */
  else                       /* It's not divisible by 4 */
    return FALSE             /* and thus not a leap year */
```

This is one way of implementing the leap year algorithm as a computer program, using the classes of statements outlined in the previous chapters. (Notice also how the comments—the text between "/*" and "*/"—makes it much easier to follow the program.)

One of the most of famous of the classic procedures is "Euclid's Algorithm," which finds the greatest common divisor for a pair of positive integers. It can be expressed as:

1) Assign the greater of the two positive integers to M and the lesser to N.

---

†"Mod" is a special operator meaning "modulo" or "remainder." For example, 11 mod 3 is 2—the remainder after 11 is divided by 3. In some languages it must be expressed as a function: mod (11, 3).

2) Divide M by N and assign the remainder (modulo) to R.

3) If R is 0, then N is the greatest common divisor. If not, then assign N to M and R to N, and repeat step 2.

Using the structured programming statements described in the previous chapters, a function to implement Euclid's algorithm could be written as

```
integer function EUCLID (x, y)
  begin
  integer r, m, n            /* defines local variables */
    if x <= 0 or
    y <= 0
      then return (−1)    /* Error: invalid integers */
    if x > y               /* Set greater, lesser */
      then
        begin
        m = x
        n = y
        end
      else
        begin
        m = y
        n = x
        end
    while (r = m mod n) > 0    /* Assign and test r */
      do
        begin
        m = n    /* Make this the new greater integer */
        n = r    /* and this is the new lesser integer */
        end      /* Now repeat the loop */
```

```
return (n)      /* Last n is the answer */
end
```

Both of these algorithms contain all of the features that Knuth defines as necessary for a successful algorithm: finiteness, definiteness, input, output, and effectiveness (Knuth 1973, 4–6).

An algorithm must be finite — it must have a beginning and an end, which occurs after a finite number of steps. The leap year algorithm makes 1, 2, or 3 decisions and then stops (it returns a final result). Euclid's algorithm divides smaller and smaller integers until the result of the division is zero, and then it too stops at that point. (An algorithm does not actually have to get into an infinite loop to fail the finiteness test; if it has a sufficiently large number of possible paths as to be impractical to follow, it is for all intents and purposes infinite.)

Each of the algorithms also has definiteness; that is, each step is precisely defined. This is part of the process of translating vague and ambiguous instructions into precise programming statements. A recipe might get away with an instruction such as "use a pinch of salt" since every cook has some understanding of what "a pinch" means, but a computer needs to know all the details and know them precisely. If every fourth century (the year 2000, for instance) is a leap year, the program needs to specify that.

The input is also precisely defined. If Euclid's Algorithm only works on positive integers greater than zero, the program must restrict input to integers within that range. The algorithm also precisely defines what its output will be: TRUE or FALSE for the leap year question; the greatest common divisor for Euclid's Algorithm.

A good algorithm is also supposed to be effective. This is a more subjective criterion than the other four, and does not always yield an optimum result. Often algorithms are comprised of choices among various techniques, none of which is perfect but which get the job done. And sometimes it is not clear that for a particular situation one algorithm is more effective or efficient than another.

Among the most common procedures, even from the early days of programming, have been functions to implement sorting algorithms. This is the type of operation for which the computer is especially suited. A simple (but by no means the most efficient) technique is to take an input list of data and create an output list that is the same size. The program scans the entire input list looking for the first element in alphabetical order, and moves that element to the top of the output list. It then repeats the process with the remaining elements until the input list is empty and the output list is full.

This approach is inefficient because it requires the program to scan the entire list over and over, once for each element in the list. It also requires double the amount of memory for each data set, since it creates a new output list equal in size to the input list. A more efficient technique (for small lists) is the *bubble sort*, which moves elements around within the array until they are all sorted:

1) Start with n as the total number of elements in the array.

2) For all elements 1 to n of the array, if any element is greater than the element that immediately follows it, exchange the two elements so that they are now in order.

3) Redefine n to be n − 1 and go back to step 2, unless n equals 1, in which case, stop. The list is now sorted.

This procedure works for lists of up to around thirty elements, after which still more sophisticated techniques are used that divide large lists into smaller pieces, sort those, and then sort the lists.[†]

Sorting algorithms have become formalized over the years and incorporated into standard libraries, and in some cases, such as COBOL, they have even been built into the language, so that all a COBOL programmer has to write is "SORT array IN ASCENDING ORDER . . ." and the compiler will generate calls to the code to perform the appropriate algorithm.

In general, traditional programming (structured or otherwise) has consisted of collections of statements that implement algorithms, each of which addresses one part of the overall problem. These collections are (in a cleanly structured program) organized into functions and function calls, retrieved from subroutine libraries, or invoked via system service calls. Other parts of the program collect the data from a terminal, file, modem, or other device, pass it on to the problem-solving sections, and report the output to the outside world in some form, be it a screen, a report, a file, or a command to a microwave heating unit to shut down.

This approach to programming has been called the "imperative" or "procedural" paradigm (Brookshear 1997, 198), meaning that the emphasis is on the commands to the computer to solve a problem and on the procedures that contain these commands. This paradigm is less concerned with the specifics of the data involved than with the techniques for manipulating that data. While it has its advantages, among them that of familiarity, it also creates difficulties in attempting to apply the same algorithm to different types of data.

An alternative approach that is currently gaining in popularity

[†]Jamsa (1985, 145–66) explains various sorting techniques in detail, and provides functions written in C to perform them.

is one that focuses on the data as much as the procedures. In this approach, the definition of the data structure incorporates the algorithms that are needed to manipulate it. In doing so, it tries to look less for similarity of algorithm than for similarity of data: how, for example, a box is like a carton or a cube, and how they are different. The data structure, its defining characteristics, and the functions associated with it are combined into a single object, which has led to this approach being called *object-oriented programming.*†

In object-oriented programming, if we want to sort a data set, we create an object that includes a sorting algorithm tailored to the specific form and contents of the data set. Similar routines are written to add an element to the list, to find an element in the list, to send the list to a disk file, and so on. Each of these routines understands the details of the list structure and components, which means that any programmer needing to use the list need not be concerned with them. When the program needs to sort the list, it invokes the "sort" function associated with the object, and the job is done for it. In addition to freeing the programmer from needing to know the object's internal structure, this packaging serves another useful purpose. If it becomes necessary to change the structure of the object—to add another type of element, for example—only the object need be changed. The programs that invoke the object would at most have to be recompiled, but no one will have to go over them and make sure that all references to the data structure have been updated—and possibly miss some in the process. This also makes object-oriented programming particularly valuable in a large project involving many programmers. While one programmer is assigned to set

†"Object" as used here has absolutely no relation to "object" as the output of a compiler.

up the internals of the data base and the routines which access it, the other members of the project team need not be aware of the details of the structure and can instead concentrate on using the data that the object supplies them.

The first object-oriented language was SIMULA, which dates back to the late 1960s. SIMULA was specifically designed to solve complex problems in computer simulations, and this specialization combined with the unfamiliarity of its techniques limited its popularity. Only in recent years has a general interest in object-orientation developed. The most popular object-oriented languages in use today are C++ (an extension of the C language) and JAVA, which somewhat resembles C. A brief examination of some of the principles they use will serve to illustrate their potential.

A programmer begins by defining a *class*, which describes the data elements (word, longword, etc.) to be contained, much as a structure does. In addition, the class definition includes the functions that will operate on the data; as part of the body of the class, the programmer writes the actual operation and control statements that will instruct the computer what to do with the data in the class. In some object-oriented languages, such as JAVA, *all* programming instructions are contained in the class definition. The principle of combining data and instructions in a single unit is called *encapsulation*, by which is meant that the data and instructions form a single "capsule" or black box. This principle prevents the programmer from accidentally passing data to a function that the latter was not intended to handle.

Defining the class does not by itself create any code or assign any space in memory; the definition is a set of instructions to the compiler on what to do when encountering an instance of the class. As an example, consider a class which defines a box: Its values are length, width, and height, and the only thing we want to know about the box is its volume. The class "box" is defined as:

```
class box
        integer length, width, height
        integer volume ( ) {
                return length * width * height
                        }
        }
```

which sets up three integer variables whose names are *length, width,* and *height.* It also defines one function, *volume,* which calculates the volume of the box and returns this calculation as its result.[†]

The next step is to define a *constructor,* which is yet another set of instructions to the compiler telling it what to do whenever a programmer makes use of this class. A constructor generally has the same name as the class and tells the compiler what data to expect and where to put it. For the class *box,* its constructor would look like this:

```
box (integer a, integer b, integer c)
    {
        length = a
        width = b
        height = c
    }
```

Whenever this constructor is used, it will set up the first param-

---

[†]Examples in this section are based on JAVA and C++, but in order to keep things simple, they do not precisely conform to the syntax of any specific language.

eter to become the length, the second to become the width, and the last parameter will be the height.

The final step is to create an actual object, which defines actual data space and creates actual code. To make life easier for the compiler (and for anyone who has to read the code), C++ and JAVA use a special reserved word "new" for this purpose:

box mycrate = new box (5,10,15)

This definition creates an object, *mycrate*, which is of the class *box* and has a length of 5, a width of 10, and a height of 15. If at some point in the code we need to know the size (that is, the volume) of this particular box, we can say:

size = mycrate.volume ()

which calls the *volume* function that was described earlier in the class definition and which will calculate the volume for this particular instance of the class of *box*.

The second principle of interest to this discussion is *inheritance*. Inheritance allows us to make a new class using a previously defined class as its basis, with additional values and functions that are specific to this variation.

Suppose we want to use a special type of box—a carton, for example. This carton has four compartments, each of which is one quarter the size of the box as a whole. We start by defining a new class:

```
class carton extends box
    {
    integer compartment ( ) {
        return (length *  width * height) / 4
                        }
    }
```

This new class, *carton*, has all of the data and functions of the class *box*—and in addition has a new function, *compartment*, which calculates the size of one compartment of the carton. When the program needs to know the size of one compartment, it will invoke the special compartment function:

compartment_size = mycarton.compartment ()

Should it need to know the size of the whole carton, that information too is available:

whole_size = mycarton.volume ()

A third principle, related to inheritance, is *polymorphism*. Here we extend the original class and *replace* some of its original parts with those that meet our specific needs. Consider a cube, for example. It is like a box except that all of its sides have identical lengths. For a cube, then, calculating its volume is simpler, and we might decide to define the class *cube* as

class cube extends box

```
{
integer volume ( ) {
    return length ∧ 3†
            }
}
```

This class redefines the *volume* function to produce the correct result for a cube rather than for the more general "box."

These examples may be trivial, but they illustrate some of the features of object orientation. In practice, objects can be ex-

†The operator "∧" is often used for exponentiation: "X ∧ Y" means "raise X to the power of Y."

tremely complex—drawing an icon on a screen, for instance—
and the ability to take an object from a general library and alter
it to fit specific needs is a powerful one indeed. Encapsulation,
inheritance, and polymorphism act to preserve all parts of the
program intact and ready for use, changing only selected portions
as necessary to solve a new problem. In a large project, one set
of programmers can be busy writing general-purpose objects,
which other programmers will then tailor to fit their own small
piece of the whole.

Objects lend themselves to organization into libraries. Once
they have been defined and tested, there is really no need for a
programmer to see their internals in order to use them; it is only
necessary to direct the compiler to the proper library where the
object definitions—the class and the constructor—are stored, and
to know how the object is to be created from them. Crafting
object libraries for C++ and JAVA programmers has already become a highly lucrative business for many software companies.

Object-orientation is no more a panacea than any other programming technique, of course. But it does take programming one
step further away from the idiosyncrasies of individual machines
and closer to the ways in which people normally look at the world.
In the example above, it allows us to think of a box, a carton, and a
cube as things that are similar but not quite identical. Where they
are the same, the program will treat them the same way, and only
those parts that are different will get different treatment. It may also
help to think of an object as yet another class of data type such as
those described in Chapter 11. Just as bytes, words, and floating
point longwords each caused the compiler to select different machine instructions to handle them, so box, carton, and cube have
their own sets of associated instructions. Ultimately an object-
oriented language becomes machine code as surely as any assem-

bler program, but for many situations it is a much more efficient way of describing the solution to a problem. In its way, object-orientation is as much a quantum leap over traditional high-level languages as compilers were over assemblers, and assembly language was over machine code.

Part IV

THE
PROGRAMMER'S
TRADE

16

THE MOTH IN THE MACHINE

In September 1944, engineers testing the Mark I computer were puzzled when a section of the circuitry suddenly began misbehaving. After several hours of furious examination, they discovered that a moth had crawled into one of the relays, preventing it from making contact. From then on, whenever the director of the Mark I project asked why something was not proceeding according to schedule, he was told it was because they were "debugging the computer." This was not the first use of "bug" to mean an error—as far back as the 1920s, telephone company repairmen referred to insulation-eating insects as "bugs in the system"—but from that moment, the terms "bug" and "debugging" came to be identified with computers and computer programming.

Bugs, or errors, are the bane of a programmer's existence. We spend most of our careers locating and fixing bugs. Maurice

Wilkes, director of the Cambridge EDSAC project, recalls the exact moment in June 1949 when, "hesitating at the angle of the stairs," he realized that "a good part of the remainder of my life was going to be spent in finding errors in my own programs."[†]

When Wilkes had his epiphany, programs were written entirely in machine and assembly language; the first compilers had not yet been invented. In the decades since, enormous amounts of ingenuity have been expended in making programs more correct and more easily correctable. Yet Wilkes's observation is by and large still true: We spend a great deal of time that could otherwise be put to productive use correcting our code.

Why this is so has to do with the precision required of programming and the complex nature of programming tasks. It is true that modern programming techniques have vastly improved our ability to find and fix bugs, but the complexity of the assignments modern programs are expected to handle has increased even faster. It is by no means uncommon for a large project to require a team of programmers working over several years and producing millions of lines of source code. In such a situation it is inevitable that some parts of the program will get in the way of others, and that one programmer will, out of habit, make use of some idiosyncrasy that another programmer is not aware of. Modifications to the design will be required, the original specifications will change, coding choices that can go either way will at different times go both ways, and so on. All of these are problems that face any large task that a group of people takes on. But when only other human beings are involved, conflicts and ambiguities can be ignored, smoothed over, even put off, in the hope that they will be forgotten. The nature of human interaction al-

---

[†]Quoted in Campbell-Kelly and Aspray (1996, 185).

lows us to cooperate even while we maintain contradictory principles and conflicting styles.

This is how we have operated throughout human history, but
what works (or at least allows us to get by) with other people is
singularly ineffective when it comes to dealing with a computer.
Ambiguities that another human being might overlook, and assumptions that other people will unconsciously accept, cannot be
tolerated in a program. The requirements for precision and accuracy, and the level of detail at which these requirements are applied, mandate far greater discipline and control than we as a
species are accustomed to accept. In an effort to achieve such precision, we have developed in the past decades any number of software techniques whose purpose is not just to make it easier to
translate algorithms into computer code but to minimize the number and types of errors we might commit in the course of doing so.

The simple advance from machine language to assembly language is the most obvious of these techniques. The development
of higher level languages is yet another step in this direction. Structured programming principles improve the accuracy and readability of the program logic, and also serve to restrict the program flow
to precise and easily traced paths. The limitations on data usage,
which restrict them to specific sections of code, serve in particular
to prevent inadvertent corruption of data. Object-oriented programming extends these principles by restricting not only access
but also operation; other parts of the program that want to manipulate a data structure do so not directly, but by invoking a function
that is associated with that structure. In addition, object-oriented
languages make it easier to manage a large project with many
programmers working simultaneously on different parts; the restrictions they impose facilitate the testing and integration of the
pieces with a greater assurance of reliability.

We have developed sophisticated tools (often called debuggers) to help us test out the program while it is still in development; these allow the programmer to step through the code, as it runs, line by line—or even machine instruction by machine instruction. When a program is in production and aborts, the operating system can provide us with its contents at the moment of failure—a *dump*—for later analysis. Sophisticated programs are also capable of analyzing themselves and reporting various abnormal conditions.

Many advances have been made in hardware as well. Even from the earliest days the circuitry had to be prepared to deal with impossible situations, such as division by zero.[†] Such an event causes a *trap* to occur—the circuitry generates an interrupt to trigger a special section of the operating system code. The trap mechanism can be used to detect a wide variety of programming errors. In particular, we can dynamically divide up the computer memory into read-write, read-only, and execute-only sections. Furthermore, we generally reserve these sections for the exclusive use of a specific program. If a program attempts to execute data as though it were code, for example, or to access a location outside of its assigned memory space, the memory management circuits will trigger a trap sequence and the operating system will be called on to deal with the access violation.

The operating system supplies the points of coordination between the hardware traps and the application program. If the programmer is running an application in test mode with a debugger active, the operating system will pass the trap back to the debugger rather than aborting the run. The programmer can then use the debugger tools to analyze just which part of the code

---

[†]In mathematics, dividing any number by zero yields infinity. However, the computer can deal only with finite numbers and so must reject a zero divisor.

triggered the trap and what can be done to correct it. (It is generally not possible, or at least not advisable, to attempt to continue execution after a trap, however!)

Although clear distinctions cannot always be drawn among them, certain programming problems may be divided into three general categories — three species of moths, as it were: syntax, semantics, and logic.

Problems in syntax are normally discovered by the assembler or compiler and quickly corrected with a simple re-edit. These are errors such as putting an operator to the left of the equal sign, leaving out the *while* part of a *do-while* loop, and so forth. The compiler, or in some cases the linker, also will identify cases of misspelled variable names — as long as they do not match some other variable name elsewhere in the program.

Some semantic errors are also recognized by the better compilers, such as a section of code that is constructed so that there is no condition under which it can be executed. More often, semantic problems are first discovered when the program has been compiled and linked and is now being tested (a stage sometimes called "unit testing," especially in a large project with many pieces in development). These sorts of errors include a properly spelled but improperly used variable — for example, writing PROFIT where LOSS was meant — or a "less than" condition where "greater than" was intended.

The latter example could also be classified as a logic error (and is also one of the most common programming bugs). Logic errors also include leaving out or incorrectly coding some part of the algorithm, such as leaving out the ELSE part of an IF-THEN-ELSE clause. Errors such as these are often quickly discovered and corrected as the program is debugged in unit testing. Sometimes errors are caught by letting the program run until it triggers a trap, such as an attempt to execute data as though it were an instruction, to write into data space that has been marked as read-only, or to read data outside of the memory assigned to the program. Other times logic errors are exposed by letting the program run to completion and comparing the results to expectations.

Logic errors can be particularly tricky to find because there are so many possible paths a program can take, and it is not physically feasible to test them all. Consider: a program that must make five decisions about data in the course of operation has, potentially, thirty-two different paths it can take ($32 = 2^5$). That means that, for the program to be thoroughly tested, all thirty-two possibilities must be exercised and checked. In practice, all thirty-two paths are seldom possible — but enough of them are to make the point that a realistic program, which must make thousands of decisions, presents something of a problem to the tester.[†] Structured and object-oriented programming techniques, properly applied, serve to reduce the number of paths that can be taken and therefore checked, but it has become accepted in the industry that no amount of testing is going to prove out every possible or even feasible variation. There will always be some unusual combination of circumstances that a tester did not think of but which some user will blithely come up with the first day a program is delivered for use ("goes live").[‡]

There are two other areas of programming difficulty, data and design, but each of these deserves a chapter of its own.

[†]A program that makes, say, a thousand different decisions, each of which might affect the others, has 2^{1000} possible decision paths. If we were test one path per second, we would still be at it when the sun goes nova — an event not anticipated until five billion years or so from now.

[‡]At one job, I came up with a maxim henceforth to be known as Kohanski's First Law of Programming: Something that has a one-in-a-million chance of going wrong will go wrong the first day we go live. To which was added Liff's Corollary: It will either happen in the first five minutes or just after everyone has left for the day.

17

THE REAL WORLD OUT THERE

Syntax, semantic, and logic problems are "pure" programming errors. In a different class—another species of moth, as it were—are problems arising at the point of intersection between the program and real world in which it must operate. This is the place where the clean logic of the computer program encounters contrary and cantankerous human beings, confronts chaotic and unpredictable phenomena, tries to extract meaningful signals from random bursts of noise.

First and foremost in this class are problems of data entry. Almost all programs operate on data that is, to some extent, outside of their control. Data may come from a file, from a keyboard entry, over a modem, or from an automatic teller machine (ATM), but what these types of data have in common is that they all ultimately come from some human source, a source that is conditioned by evolution and training to communicate with other human beings and not with inanimate machines. We are not always precise in our dealings, nor do we expect this to cause us much difficulty; if the person listening does not quite understand, we can always add some more explanation.

This ability to live in a world of ambiguities and imprecision, of multiple alternatives for one word and multiple meanings for another, is a skill we learned as children without even thinking about it. It is, however, a skill the computer knows nothing about, except where the programmer is conscientious enough to build the equivalent of years of childhood training into the program—and even then it is, at best, a pale shadow of what for the average seven-year-old has already become a natural skill.

An illustration of this problem comes from a system that Blue Cross and Blue Shield of Wisconsin tried to put in place in 1983 for paying insurance claims. At one point a data entry clerk responded to a computer question by entering "none"—something another human being would have instantly understood. The computer, however, proceeded to send out hundreds of checks addressed to the "town" of None, Wisconsin. Overpayments and duplicate checks also plagued the system (Lee 1991, 115).

It is unrealistic to expect general users and even trained computer operators to be held to the same standards of precision that professional programmers are expected to meet, all the more so when programmers themselves so rarely achieve them. The programmer thus has two major responsibilities in preparing data entry code: first, to ensure that the entry is a valid one; and second, since no program can cover all such possibilities, to provide a means for correcting data that has been entered incorrectly.

There are many ways of controlling the way data is entered

into a computer. An operator may be given a list of specified items—a menu—and required to choose one only, in a pull-down menu controlled by mouse clicks, for example. Character data may be cut off after a prescribed number of keystrokes, limited to decimal numbers in a certain range, and so on. Where a user needs to enter random alphabetic data of indeterminate length, the program may validate it against a list of known possibilities for that data; thus, in the example above, "none" would have been rejected because it was not on a set list of cities. Similarly, a bank payment entry system is programmed to reject an order to send money to a bank whose name it cannot find in its list of correspondents.

Of course, this passion for correctness can be carried too far; if the good citizens of Wisconsin had indeed incorporated a new city by the name of None and no one had gotten around to updating the computer database yet, there would be a very frustrated operator trying desperately to convince an even more stubborn computer that such a city really did exist. To allow for this, the program could ask the operator to verify the name, and if this really is a new city or town in Wisconsin, it would ask whether the new name should be added to the database. Think also of a spellchecker, which is loaded with a collection of commonly known words, and to which the user adds accepted variants, proper names, and so forth in the course of usage.

This kind of adaptable database may not work so well in the bank example, but here, too, allowance can be made for the varieties of ways by which different people will identify the same object. If a program can identify "Banco di Roma," "BNK Roma," and "The Bank of Rome" as all being the same institution, then it is learning to live in the real world.

Another form of data that the computer must contend with is

that gathered by mechanical instruments, often called telemetry data. The problem here is that such data is initially gathered in analog form — that is, as continuous movement — rather than discrete digital signals. A seismograph will register an earthquake by making movements with a stylus, and these movements must be converted into digital values before a computer can interpret them, a process that is subject to vagaries of equipment, temperature, humidity, and many other uncontrollable and often momentary conditions.

Data transmission is also a potent source of problems. A weather satellite may monitor a storm path, and the telemetry data it sends back to Earth must pass through that same storm or other atmospheric disturbances, must have sunspot activity filtered out, and so on — and still is expected to provide enough useful and recognizable data that a program can make sense of it. Computer programs need to be aware both of spurious signals and of missing bits and pieces and be able to extract the maximum amount of useful information from unreliable sources. In this area, too, one can err too much on the side of caution. It is possible that we would have become aware of the growing hole in the ozone layer many years ago, except that back in 1979, when the NASA satellites that first observed the problem reported their readings, the numbers were so far off the expected norms that the computer programs which were to process the data rejected them as being telemetry errors (Forester and Morrison 1994, 118).[†]

A related type of data transmission is that sent from one computer to another; this is known as *telecommunications*. In addition

---

[†]After British scientists in the mid-1980s announced that ground observations showed a hole in the ozone layer, NASA reexamined the raw satellite data from as far back as 1979 and discovered that the hole had indeed been reported correctly all along.

to dealing with the problems of telemetry that can occur with noise on the line and breaks in transmission, each of the two computers must be in agreement as to how the data is to be formatted — they must agree on the message *protocol*. This is a set of standards describing what kinds of messages are to be sent, how the data is to be laid out, at what point receipt of the message is to be acknowledged, how missing messages will be handled, and so on. Over the years communications systems developers have crafted wildly different and sometimes mutually exclusive protocols, which may have met their specific requirements but also cause difficulties in the industry at large. Various business, national, and international committees over the years have attempted to promote their own standards, such as SWIFT and X.400, but these are not universal and do not meet every need. Programs that send and receive messages to and from other computers need to be prepared to deal with unexpected data and odd combinations, even though they are communicating with programs written by other professionals.

Programs not only need the capacity to weed out incorrectly received data while accepting valid readings, they also need the flexibility to correct data entries later on. Despite all our best efforts, there is no program that can spot, for example, a grocery store cashier's error in charging $20.00 when $2.00 was meant; both entries are reasonable purchases. But the alert customer who spots the mistake, or who later brings the problem to the manager, should not be held hostage to a programmer's oversight in neglecting to allow for human error. While an $18.00 overcharge may not be life-threatening, real-life stories of government computers declaring someone deceased and refusing to accept information to the contrary show that such an oversight can be of more consequence than we might like to believe. Every now and then yet another horror story surfaces in the press of someone who is mistakenly identified by a police computer as a criminal and arrested, and then arrested again and again because the criminal tracking program included no provision for expunging mistakes, or because the mistake was corrected in one computer but there was no part of the program that would inform the rest of the crime-tracking network. In each of these cases, the computer's aura of infallibility poses an ethical challenge for the programmer. True, there is a potential for abuse in allowing arrest records to be changed, but the cost of building in safeguards against abuse is far less than the cost to individuals and to society of not providing any corrective means at all. Programmers must always keep in mind that their programs are going to be used by fallible human beings.

The necessity for programs to validate and repair data entries is only one facet of the larger problem of enabling people and computers to work together in something approaching harmony. Consideration must be given to how the program will be used, the way in which it appears to the user, the manner in which it displays information, and the process of collecting input. This process is often known as human engineering (or sometimes ergonomics), though it has also been called "user-centered design" (Landauer 1995, 205–36). A programmer trying to market a new piece of PC software who has not thought this aspect through may end up with a product that languishes on the shelf. More seriously, critical applications that confuse or discourage the operators who must work with them can cause all kinds of havoc, sometimes with fatal consequences. When the USS Vincennes shot down an Iran Air passenger plane in 1988, killing all 290 on board, it was in large part because the Aegis computer system tracking the plane displayed critical information on two different consoles, thus confusing crewmen in an already tense combat situation. Subsequent analysis of the computer tapes showed that all the information needed to identify the plane as a civilian airliner was there, but that it was not clearly presented on the screens (Forester and Morrison 1994, 109).

Programmers too often have a habit of writing programs to do things the way they personally find obvious and comfortable. What is obvious to someone trained in the rigors of computer logic, however, may be simply bewildering to a user or even an experienced operator who does not understand the internals of a program. This can lead to cryptic messages such as, for example, "MALFUNCTION 54" instead of "radiation overdose."[†] It may be that some of this confusion in interpreting the messages from our computers is an aspect of the current generation of users, which is the generation of transition between the world of paper and the world of terminal screens. The generations to come will have been raised on computers from childhood, and will have a trained instinct for both the expressiveness and the limitations of a display of information (and for those that cannot get this training, it will become yet one more piece of evidence of the growing gap between the rich and the poor). Even so, the human race will never escape its use of ambiguities, its assumptions, or the limits of how quickly we can absorb critical information. It remains the programmer's responsibility to validate data entry on input, and to make a proper presentation of the output.

[†]"Malfunction 54" was the complete text of an actual message that appeared on a Therac-25 console, a machine used for radiation therapy. The operator, not understanding what it meant, tried resetting a few buttons, which apparently cleared the condition. But the machine delivered a huge overdose, and several patients died from radiation poisoning (Lee 1991, 9).

The chaotic nature of data input, and the caution required in presenting it as output, are only parts of the fundamental discrepancy that exists between the precise, binary interior of the computer and the real, analog world. Inside the computer, data is ultimately represented by ones and zeros, truth and falsity; an item either is or it is not. The idea of the world as a series of truths and falsehoods is a very old one in Western thinking, and goes back at least as far as Aristotle, 2,500 years ago. Aristotle held that a thing either is or is not, has a quality or does not have it, with no position in between. The sky is either blue or it is not-blue. A man is either tall or not-tall. Aristotle's system of syllogistic logic is built on the principle of the excluded middle: Nothing can be both A and not-A.

The real world, however, is much more ambiguous, as can be seen from some of the examples given earlier in this chapter. This has long posed a problem for logicians trying to construct a model of the real world using the certainties of Aristotle. In this century, philosophers such as Russell and Black have offered the concept of vagueness and the use of multivalued logic as alternatives to Aristotle's bivalued or binary logic, and in 1965, Lotfi Zadeh, in a continuation of Russell's thinking, published a paper proposing a new system that he called "fuzzy logic," which could be applied to computers.

In Zadeh's system, things are neither A nor not-A, but somewhere in between. On a scale of 0 to 1, objects will have values such as 0.1 or 0.5. For example, consider the quality of tallness. Rather than saying that a person is tall or not-tall, we assign a unit of tallness, 0.6, to a particular height, say five foot nine. A person of that height is thus tall to 0.6 degree, which gives a numerical value to the vague human term "somewhat tall."

Some have argued that fuzzy logic is really just probability in disguise, but this is not correct. A person who is five foot nine does not have a 0.6 probability of being tall; he *is* tall to a degree of 0.6. But the confusion of fuzziness with probability, as well as Western science's adherence to Aristotelian bivalued logic, have made it difficult for fuzzy logic to win acceptance here.[†]

Despite its name, however, fuzzy logic is not imprecise. Once the categories and their values have been established (a process dependent on the programmer's experience and gut feeling as much as anything else, perhaps), application of fuzzy logic principles are as precise as any other computer operation. While the algorithms thus constructed are more complex than in a bivalued logic environment, they still meet Knuth's requirements of precision.

As an example of how fuzzy logic can be used in computer programs, consider a database of a company's salespeople. Suppose we want to make a list of all new employees who have good sales records. Both "new" and "good" are vague terms that a human being could easily apply but which are hard for a computer to grasp. If we were to assign a value of, say, six months to the concept of "new," then a computer program using Aristotelian logic would skip over an employee who had been there for six months and a day. The employee is either new or not-new. This approach also misses employees who may not have sold much in dollar terms but who have only been there for a month.

In a fuzzy logic approach, we would assign different values to different stages of "new," so that the first month would be 1, the second month 0.8, and so on until after six months, the value of "new" would be zero. We would assign similar values for dollar

†Zadeh's choice of terms only adds to the difficulty. Bart Kosko, Zadeh's student and perhaps principle disciple, comments that Zadeh "chose the word 'fuzzy' to spit in the eye of modern science" (Kosko 1993, 20).

amounts to be units of "good" and then use various fuzzy techniques to determine whether the combination of the two values yields a result that passes the fuzzy criteria of new employees with good sales records.

Fuzzy logic also has applications in real-time systems, which must constantly adjust to changing conditions. The subway system in Sendai, Japan, is run by computers using microchips built with fuzzy logic circuits, and is generally considered the smoothest ride in the world (McNeill and Freiberger 1993, 144). Another area where fuzzy logic is proving useful is in "expert systems"—programs that try to duplicate the reasoning of an expert, such as a physician, so that a computer can analyze a patient's symptoms and produce a diagnosis. Classical artificial intelligence techniques have made little headway here; a physician relies on trained intuition, hunches, and experience far more than on clear-cut rules, and these are not easily reduced to Aristotelian syllogisms. Fuzzy logic provides a much closer approximation of how a physician really thinks.

Fuzzy logic is not for every situation, of course. A bank account does not contain "a lot of money"; it contains an exact amount. A bank program that conducts risk analysis, however, is a candidate for a fuzzy logic approach. Fuzzy logic does not completely overcome the problem of representing a continuous, analog world as a set of discrete digital numbers, but it is a major advance in bringing together the certainties of the computer and the chaos of the world.

ENIAC co-inventor J. Presper Eckert (center) and Walter Cronkite of CBS television (right) review output from UNIVAC I, a direct descendant of ENIAC technology, predicting the results of the 1952 U.S. presidential election. This was the first time a computer was used for predicting election results. UNIVAC I predicted that Eisenhower would defeat Stevenson by 438 electoral votes to 93; the actual count was 442 to 89 in favor of Eisenhower. However, CBS refused to broadcast the prediction, believing that the sample used by UNIVAC I was too small for the results to be reliable. *(Photo and caption courtesy of UNISYS Corporation.)*

The Williams tube (top) and the mercury delay line (below) were among the earliest devices used for memory storage. The mercury delay line preserved its state (one or zero) by generating a sound pulse that traveled through a column of mercury to a receiver at the other end. The delay caused by the passage through the mercury was enough to make the state reusable. Some early UNIVAC computers were built with mercury delay line memory.

The Williams tube used an electron beam to mark a spot on the phosphor screen, either high (one) or low (zero). Until the phosphor faded, it could be read repeatedly. When it was first unveiled for public view, the photographers' flash bulbs excited the entire screen at once, causing memory failure. The IBM 702 computers, built around 1950, used some Williams tubes. *(Smithsonian Institution photos No. 78-6622 [Williams tube] and 91-10380 [mercury delay line]. Photos courtesy of the Smithsonian Institution.)*

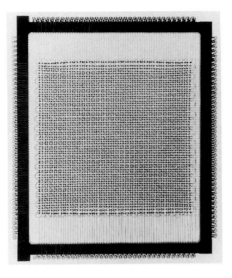

Magnetic cores woven into a plane were the standard memory circuit from the 1950s into the early 1970s. Each core was a doughnut-shaped magnet that held a positive or negative charge (one or zero). Some of the wires threaded through the hole identified its location in memory, while others read or wrote the charge.

The small ceramic square in the bottom of the lower photo was the first commercial all-semiconductor memory module. It consisted of four chips holding a total of 512 bits, more than all the cores in the same photo. A modern memory chip of the same size (one half-inch square) holds more than a million bits. *(Photos courtesy of IBM archives.)*

The IBM 1620 was first produced in 1959. The central panel lights are for diagnostic purposes, but I remember being able to tell by watching them when the computer was executing a multiply instruction. The operator is holding a removable disk pack and standing in front of the disk drive. To her right is a plotter, and beyond that a printer; to its left is the card reader and punch. Cards were the primary means of programming the 1620, although it was possible to type machine instructions directly into the console typewriter. The IBM 1620 was perhaps the only computer to use decimal (actually, binary-coded decimal) machine language. *(Photo courtesy of IBM archives.)*

Assigned GO TO Statements		One modification of the GO TO statement which allows greater freedom in directing the logical flow of a program is the assigned GO TO statement. The assigned GO TO statement requires a companion statement, an ASSIGN statement, which must be previously executed.	

As an example of the use of the assigned GO TO statement, suppose it is desired to calculate several average values such as average temperature, pressure, and density. If the data is on cards, the following program might be used:

C ◄ FOR COMMENT / STATEMENT NUMBER			FORTRAN STATEMENT
			DIMENSION X(25)
5			ASSIGN 30 TO N
10			READ 2, X
			SUM = 0.0
15			DO 20 I = 1, 25
20			SUM = SUM + X(I)
25			AVG = SUM/25.0
26			GO TO N, (30, 40, 50)
30			AVGTEM = AVG
31			ASSIGN 40 TO N
			GO TO 10
40			AVGPRE = AVG
41			ASSIGN 50 TO N
			GO TO 10
50			AVGDEN = AVG
			PRINT 60, AVGTEM, AVGPRE, AVGDEN
			STOP
60			FORMAT (3E14.5)

In this example, statement 26 transfers control to one of the three statements referred to in the list, i.e., 30, 40 or 50, depending upon the value of N at the time of execution, which is determined by the last preceding ASSIGN statement. The first execution of statement 26 causes control to be transferred to statement 30, since statement 5, the last preceding ASSIGN statement, assigned the value of 30 to N. Statement 31 assigns the value of 40 to N; hence the second execution of statement 26 transfers control to statement 40. The third execution of statement 26 transfers control to statement 50, the value of 50 having been assigned to N by statement 41.

In general terms, the assigned GO TO statement is written

$$GO\ TO\ N,\ (n_1,\ n_2,\ \ldots,\ n_m)$$

where N is a non-subscripted integer variable appearing in a previously executed ASSIGN statement, and n_1, n_2, $\ldots$, n_m stand for statement numbers. These statement numbers are, in effect,

A page from the first IBM FORTRAN manual published in 1957. The manual is still considered a classic because of its easy explanations and clear text. This page explains a FORTRAN construction called "assigned GOTO," which is similar to the "switch" construction in structured programming, although it is much less tightly controlled. *(Photo courtesy of IBM archives.)*

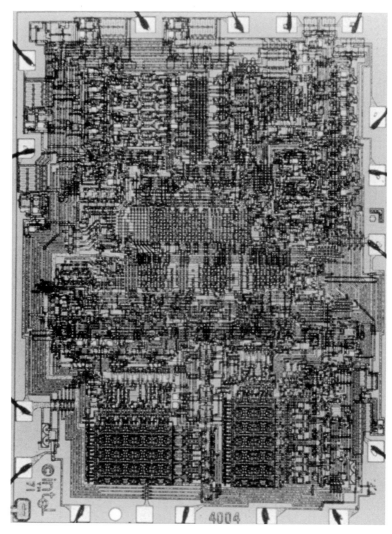

The circuitry of an Intel 4004 chip. The world's first microprocessor, it was designed for Intel by Marcian E. Hoff in 1971. The chip contained the equivalent of around 5,000 transistors and measured less than two inches square. *(Photo courtesy of Intel Corporation.)*

The Intel Pentium® Pro microprocessor. A product of the mid-1990s, this chip holds over 5 million transistors in a space measuring and inch-and-a-half square. The Pentium series of computer chips are the most popular on the market today. A set of Pentium Pro microprocessors connected in parallel was recently able to achieve a speed of 1 trillion floating-point instructions per second. *(Photo courtesy of Intel Corporation.)*

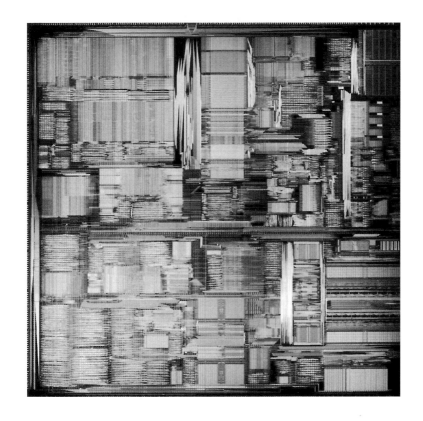

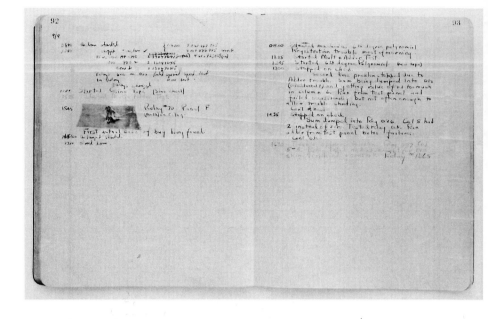

This page from Grace Hopper's logbooks on the Harvard Mark I, dated September 9, 1944, preserves the moth that crawled into a relay and shorted it out, causing the computer to produce erroneous results. After several hours of fruitless testing, engineers discovered the "bug" in the circuitry, and Col. Hopper taped it into her log. Thereafter, whenever Howard Aiken, the project director, would ask why some procedure was taking so long, he would be told it was because they were "debugging the computer." "Bugs" and "debugging" are still terms favored by computer programmers. *(Smithsonian Institution Photo No. 92-13131. Photo courtesy of the Smithsonian Institution.)*

18

THE LIMITATIONS OF DESIGN

There remains yet one more species of "moth," so to speak: the problems arising from design. Even after all the syntax and semantics errors have been resolved, after all the logic paths have been traced and fixed, after the program has been improved to accept only valid data and to display its output neatly, there remains the issue of the program itself: Did we really want it to do the things we designed it to do?

The problems discussed in the previous chapter that arise from failing to consider the user's perception of the application are examples of the limitations of design. Programmers often plan a program's display according to what interests them and use layouts that they personally find useful, never stopping to consider that most users never see the inside of a program; nor do they approach it the way a programmer does. What makes perfect sense to a computer expert may be gibberish to even a trained user ("malfunction 54" is a case in point).

Inviting the users to participate in the design process is often seen as a way of avoiding this pitfall, but users can create as many design problems as they solve by their participation. Particularly when the project is large and intended for a specific client or institution, it is to be expected that users will request and even demand major changes in the design. Some of this is understandable; when a project is a number of years in development and installation, it is inevitable that new requirements will be discovered and old requirements dropped. External forces, such as regulatory agencies, also may impose new features by force of law, and the law of the market adds a powerful incentive as well. Managers will come and go, and the new manager may insist on doing things differently than the old one did. Programmers themselves may also find it necessary or desirable to change an approach as the coding and testing phase reveals unexpected complications, or as the team changes and the new programmers bring different idiosyncrasies to the job.

A designer will try to anticipate these midstream changes and build in the flexibility to handle them, but no one can anticipate everything. What happens then, especially when the project is well along, is that some code will be bent to fit the new requirements and some will be left alone. As a result, such midproject changes often result in what is called "spaghetti code" — programs whose flow of execution resembles nothing so much as a bowl of spaghetti strands going in all directions. This kind of situation is, as it were, a breeding ground for moths.

Modular programming was developed partly in an attempt to minimize the effect of design alterations, and object-oriented programming is a further, deliberate step in this direction. Of course properly used comments are essential as well. But even the best modular techniques cannot eliminate subtleties of interaction among the parts of the program, and many of the data structures will also have been designed to work together in a specific way. There is no panacea and no perfect solution.

On occasion an application will become so overloaded with changes, corrections, and updates that it would be better to scrap it and start afresh with a new program using the latest techniques. But this requires a heavy investment in a project that may not be usable for years; in the meantime the old version (the "legacy system") must be kept running, even upgraded from time to time. It is often difficult to persuade management to replace a system that is working, however clumsily. Thus it happens that applications that were hastily planned as temporary fixes often end up being the foundation of programs still in use years, even decades, later.

This is part of the reason behind one the classic failures of design in the history of computers: the year 2000 problem. This was presented earlier as a failure of aesthetics, which is an aspect of design, but it is a failure of management as well. Although we have been aware for some time of the approaching new century, force of habit, both in programming and in real life, as well as a tendency to reuse existing programs and data structures, have fostered a situation in which many programmers continued to assign a two-digit field to the year. Even after programmers began to notice the potential for a year 2000 disaster, management proved reluctant to deal with or even listen to their concerns: After the first known published warning about this problem appeared in ComputerWorld magazine (in 1984), the author was fired for irritating his managers too often on the subject (Ulrich and Hayes 1997, 5).

Another design that did not anticipate its current use is the ARPAnet. Originally conceived by the Defense Advanced Research Projects Agency (DARPA, later changed to ARPA), the ARPAnet was intended to link the research communities — universities and some government agencies — together in a way that would allow for the improved communication of ideas. Now, it is essential to a functioning academic environment that this be a *free* exchange of ideas and information, without control or censorship. Ideas must be left alone to survive or fail in the arena of peer judgment, and new and better ideas often arise out of the synthesis of many different thoughts interacting and colliding with each other. The ARPAnet was expected to grow into the global expansion of the academicians' ideal forum.

This indeed it has become, as much as it is possible for any human institution to approach its ideal. But in the process, the ARPAnet — since renamed the Internet — also attracted the attention of commercial interests for whom information is not something to be freely exchanged but rather a commodity to be offered for a fee. The resulting conflict between design and application has yet to be resolved, and demonstrates how the unanticipated consequences of a design may raise ethical as well as aesthetic concerns.

Offering information for sale means not only that proprietary information must somehow be secured in what was meant to be an open environment, but also that the means of payment must be protected.

Users are reluctant to offer credit card information when they have reason to suspect that it may be captured or distributed to unauthorized parties who will then run up charges at their expense. While this problem also exists in the regular marketplace, the impermeability of computer programs (and the transportability and reproducibility of computer information) make it that much harder to maintain the security of payment authorizations.

When information becomes a commodity, it also creates the temptation to acquire more of it to sell. Web sites that offer information may also collect it, generally unbeknownst to the hapless user, and then package the collection for sale to direct marketing companies to use in targeted advertising. The rise in junk e-mail—unsolicited offers of information, goods, and services—has become such a concern in the Internet community as to raise the prospect of legislation to curb it, while private information, such as assets, social security numbers, and relationship entanglements, have proven to be irresistible targets for gossips and thieves.

Similarly, databases stored on corporate and government computers that have links to the Internet are an invitation to the unscrupulous. A whole industry has arisen to create "firewalls" that limit access to these corporate and government databases, but another, underground, community has sprung up that is devoted to defeating these protections. It is proving almost impossible to suppress them completely, largely because of the openness of the original ARPAnet design.

The open Internet has also attracted purveyors of pornography, which in turn has led for calls to censor the Internet. American attempts to do so have so far been ruled unconstitutional; in any case such censorship will ultimately prove impractical, given the proliferation of Internet sites around the world, accessible to all yet beyond the legal reach of would-be censors and their compliant governments. Such a situation has its advantages as well as disadvantages; the attempted coup against Mikhail Gorbachev in the waning days of the Soviet Union failed in large measure because his allies and defenders were able to use the Internet and other means of communication to keep the outside world aware of what was happening. To the extent that the uncontrollable Internet can frustrate the designs of tyrants who need secrecy in which to operate, it is succeeding beyond the wildest dreams of academe.

Another gap between the Internet's design and its use is its inability to establish the identity of its participants and to prevent them from abusing or overusing the facilities. Because the Internet (or more precisely, its predecessor, the ARPAnet) was designed without a central control, each institution connected to the Internet was expected to control its users and their access to the community at large. When the ARPAnet was confined to the academic and research world, it was taken for granted that these institutions would be accountable for their members and would limit access to those who use it responsibly. Commercial institutions, however, have no incentive to limit or control their subscribers' access; on the contrary, it is in their interest to have as many subscribers using their facilities as often and as uninhibitedly as possible.

If a message generates controversy, that in turn generates more messages in response (sometimes called a "flame war"), and each new message brings in more revenue.† Nor are commercial Web sites always as careful about preserving the integrity of identity; there are even some that earn their fees by concealing the true identity of a sender. The misuse and overuse of the Internet have reached the point that elements of the original ARPAnet community have suggested creating a completely new, strictly academic network separate from the Internet world.

Even more examples of the limitations of design can be found in programming languages themselves. The first high-level lan-

---

†Some commercial providers do make an effort to monitor their internal forums to keep things from getting out of hand, but even these institutions have neither the ability nor the desire to discipline misuse of the Internet at large.

guages were conceived and crafted mainly in response to external considerations. FORTRAN was designed with the goal of demonstrating that a compiler program could produce machine code that was as fast and efficient as any written by a good assembly language programmer. A secondary aim was to make it easier to translate mathematical formulas into computer terms. The result was a language that, while it produced efficient code, was somewhat limited in its applicability. The need for compiler speed also forced restrictions such as limits on the size of a variable name and on the number of dimensions allowed in an array; maneuvering around these restrictions could result in a program that was difficult to understand.

COBOL, on the other hand, had as one of its primary goals ease of readability by managers who knew nothing of computers. As a result, the designers created a language that was cumbersome to use and often slow in execution. Moreover, the emphasis on code pseudoreadability fostered a mistaken belief that comments could be minimalized or even done away with altogether, the result being a whole collection of COBOL programs that neither manager nor programmer could easily follow.

Unlike structured programming languages such as ALGOL and C, and object-oriented ones such as JAVA, neither FORTRAN nor COBOL makes any attempt to enforce limits on data access, so any data structure in the program is, for all intents and purposes, available to be manipulated by any section of code. This situation invites errors of inadvertent encroachment of data, errors that can be difficult to find because any part of the program could be at fault.

Many of these problems were recognized fairly early in the lifespan of these languages, but by then a whole user community had sprung up and a multitude of applications had been created.

(To this day, more lines of code have been written in FORTRAN and COBOL than in any other language.) The investment in existing programs and in language training meant that any attempt to improve the language had to be undertaken so as not to invalidate already existing code; in other words, any advances in the languages had to maintain *backwards compatibility*. This requirement places a limit on the degree to which original design flaws can be corrected.

Similarly, the design goal of *portability* has proven to be effectively impossible to attain. One of the ideas behind the first high-level languages was that a program should be portable — that is, it should be possible to take a program written on one computer platform (the hardware and operating system) and run it on any other platform with no more effort than recompiling and relinking it for the new machine. But each platform has its unique properties that are either missing or in conflict with other platforms. Moreover, these properties are features that programmers may want to use, such as specific means of accessing a tape or disk file. Computer manufacturers also sometimes try to develop customer loyalty by offering their own editions of COBOL, FORTRAN, and other languages, which provide functions that other versions do not have. Some attempts at standardization have been made but, again, backward compatibility is an issue here. Newer languages such as C have attempted to achieve something close to portability by insisting on a minimalist approach, but any time a program uses a system service unique to the platform, or does more than the simplest input or output (another system service), its chances of being portable drop dramatically. The JAVA language hopes to get around this problem by providing "virtual machines," a set of programs that are each specific to some real machine platform. The JAVA program itself runs on the virtual machine, and thus behaves identically regardless of which real machine is using it. Although JAVA has become very popular, it is still quite new. It is too soon to tell whether this technique will guarantee true portability, or whether human nature's insistence on tinkering with the various implementations will defeat this design as well.

But the single most influential design decision in the history of computers is the one made back in the beginning: to adopt a single-threaded, serial processing technique, which is still known today as a "von Neumann machine."

The earliest computers — the Colossus, the ENIAC, and their mechanical predecessors — were constructed as parallel processors. That is, they could perform more than one operation simultaneously, by distributing the task among several subprocessors that ran independently. The Colossus used five processors in parallel, each one running a tape at 5,000 characters a second, using electron tubes called Thyratrons to keep them synchronized, while the ENIAC used an internal electric clock as a cycling device to control the flow among its thirty or so units (Ritchie 1986, 95–96, 160).

When the EDVAC was being designed during World War II, various people on the project, particularly John von Neumann, argued that the machine could be so fast that parallel processing and the cumbersome coordinations it required would be unnecessary:

> The device should be as simple as possible; that is, it should contain as few elements as possible. This can be achieved by never performing two operations simultaneously, if this would cause a significant increase in the number of elements required. The result will be that the device will work more re-

liably and the vacuum tubes can be driven to shorter reaction times than otherwise (von Neumann First Draft, §5.6. Printed in Stern 1981, 192–93).

Rather than perform several operations at once as its predecessors had done, the EDVAC executed one machine instruction at a time. This method does avoid the problem of coordinating operations, a difficulty that previous computers partially ignored by focusing on a limited repertoire of special operations, but which would grow exponentially in a general purpose computer running stored programs that could change dynamically. Von Neumann and the EDVAC crew opted to avoid the problem altogether. The resulting serial, single-step computer, though much refined and adjusted, is the model for almost all computers in use today. The interrupt mechanism allows for portions of the hardware to operate in parallel — that is, independently of the rest of the computer — and other advances in memory management have speeded up the process of selecting the next instruction, but the computer's instruction circuits still will not execute the next machine instruction until they have completed the previous one.

While it is true that vacuum tubes, which in 1945 were state of the art, were fast enough to solve the problems von Neumann had in mind, the limitations imposed by the von Neumann structure prevent even the fastest computers now existing from solving today's much more complicated problems. We are developing formulas, for example, for use in attempting to predict the weather. They may never make the weather completely predictable, but even in their current state they are so complex that when we apply them one calculation at a time, our computers are simply not fast enough to finish the job before the weather actually happens.

Weather problems provide an ideal candidate for parallel processing. But the complexities of communication among the parallel processors that defeated von Neumann continue to plague designers today. Not long ago, an experimental computer consisting of a few hundred microprocessors in parallel achieved a speed of a trillion instructions a second. This sounds impressive until one realizes that it could not do so every second, but only in those instants when all of the processors had been assigned their proper programs and given their part of the data to work on. As each processor completed its assignment, it had to wait until all the others had completed theirs, or in some other way coordinated their activities so as to sustain a meaningful speed of operation. It is an arguable but ultimately unanswerable contention that we would by now have solved the problem of parallel processor synchronization had von Neumann not given up in frustration; certainly there were those at the time who thought so.[†] The potential of parallel processing continues to attract attention from computer scientists and manufacturers, but so far the von Neumann model is still the order of the day.

Errors in design, failures to design, insufficient attention to design — all of these are faults that have plagued humanity since the first group of hunters tried to organize a mastodon kill. But as with everything else it touches, the computer magnifies our human failings, even to the point where a single programmer's design flaw can cause repercussions around the world.

[†]Derrick Henry Lehmer, who in 1926 invented an electro-mechanical parallel processing computer that produced prime numbers, was known for complaining that the decision to go with serial processing had ruined computers (Ritchie 1986, 180).

19

PROGRAMMING AS ABSTRACTION

AND REFLECTION

All language is an abstraction of the real world. By finding words that to one degree or another approximately correspond to our ideas and experiences, we are able to express ourselves to other people whose understanding of these same words is close enough to our own that we can be reasonably confident we have communicated something of what we mean. We are able to use words to do this because words organize the phenomena of the world into classes: the class of chairs is separate from the class of tables is distinct from the class of desks. We classify colors as red or orange, green or blue. We divide people into categories as well: tall and short; fat and thin; black, white, Asian, Amerindian.

Inevitably, these classes are only approximations of the real world, and users of the terms do not always agree on what they mean. The Japanese concept of "aoi" is not quite the same as what the English word means by "blue." Is a person who has one black ancestor, four generations back, white or black — or something in between? How heavy does a person have to be in order to be "fat," and in what proportion to height and age? Where is the line between "thin" and anorexic? Are these categories fixed, or do they change over time as the person's self-awareness changes? When does a table become a desk? No matter how many words we define or use to account for the varieties of objects and ideas we encounter, at some point we have to sacrifice precision and accept a degree of vagueness sufficient to encompass most of the members we wish to include in the category, without excluding too many of those that might in fact belong.

Mathematics is the ultimate abstraction; it reduces all objects to numerical constructs that can then be compared to other numerical constructs for similarity and identity. Such a number is precise and has an exact meaning, but it does not reflect the way in which we relate to the world. In what amounts to a reversal of the necessities of language, mathematics at some point sacrifices vagueness in order to achieve precision.

Consider a heap of sand. It contains a countable number of grains, although we do not ask what that number is in order to decide that it is a heap. Remove one grain, and it remains a heap. Remove another grain, and yet another, until only one grain is left. That final grain is not a heap, but at what point did the collection of grains of sand lose the quality of "heapness?" No mathematical formula gives us the answer. There is a vagueness about the concept of "heap," as there is about the concept of "table" or "black" or "thin," that is not reducible to a number.

A program is an abstraction of the programmer's thoughts on how to interpret and manipulate the real world. But it must run on a computer, which is a construct that obeys the laws of mathematics; when thought is translated into program it loses the ability to live with vagueness that thought employs. At some point the program must return an answer—a precise but incomplete approximation of the real world. Even if the programmer follows the principles of fuzzy logic and assigns degrees of a quality to an object, those assignments are themselves discrete numbers and thus in themselves approximations.

The digital computer actually takes abstraction one step beyond pure mathematics; as was pointed out in Chapter 6, the computer representation of numbers does not permit an infinity of points. No matter how fine a distinction we construct, inevitably we will confront two numbers that are next to one another with no number in between. The object in the real world might be better described as being between these two discrete numbers, but the computer must approximate its value as being one or the other.

In spite of this limitation, the closeness of these approximations, and the power of the computer to manipulate numbers and the information they represent, have increasingly led us to accept the mathematicization of information as a major influence on our lives. The reduction of phenomena to numbers that fit into the orderly structures of mathematics also seduces us into believing we can avoid the unruly and chaotic real world. But the raw material of thought is information, and to the extent that we accept computer-digested data instead of seeking it on our own, our ideas about the world are based on incomplete approximations filtered through some programmer's judgment calls and the limitations of the machine.

The Census Bureau, in its decennial survey of the American population, includes a question asking for the race of each respondent. There is always a debate over which categories to include and whether to allow a combination of categories so as to permit people of mixed ancestry to describe themselves more accurately. No matter how the questionnaire is constructed, however, some people will protest that it does not cover their own situations—they fall between the discrete points that the questionnaire defines.

Clearly, any survey has to set such discrete categories, but when such a survey's categorizations are magnified by the computer it becomes easier to overlook the infinite gradations of humanity and accept the computer's divisions instead. Now, this degree of racial precision that the computer program presents is set by the programmer, even if in consultation with or at the orders of the persons paying for the product. The working program is thus the abstraction of someone's thoughts on what race means, which are further constrained by the limits of the computer's capacity and the programmer's skill. Yet the reports that these census programs produce have a major impact on where our legislators will come from and where our money goes. To a greater extent than we realize, this impact is guided not by Congress or the Secretary of Commerce but by anonymous programmers expressing their thoughts in the languages of the computer.

The ability of anonymous clerks and technicians to influence the decisions of the rulers did not begin with the computer, of course. But the amount of the information that the computer can process, and the complexity and impermeability of the programs that enable it to do so, increase these technicians' influence exponentially while at the same time making it all the more difficult to hold them accountable. So we are inclined to accept as fact a statement from the computer that there are x number of people in this country of a certain race; that so-and-so is living or dead; that there is an outstanding warrant for someone's arrest.

We have reduced human beings to a computerized abstraction that might indeed be neat and orderly but also may well be inaccurate, and in any case is woefully incomplete.

We can live with this sort of reduction only as long as we bear in mind that it *is* nothing more than an incomplete representation of the real people and the real world; while it may be necessary, it is not sufficient. Our inability to break people down into their constituent parts and describe them exactly to a computer should not be used as an excuse to deal only with those parts we can describe, even though dealing with such an approximation is neater and easier than dealing with the real thing. Each of us has an element of vagueness that, though impossible to digitize, is part of the essence of our humanity.

Our ability to abstract our thoughts into computer programs is limited not only by the impossibility of translating vagueness into precision, but also because we do not really understand how we think. Much of the thinking process takes place at the subconscious level, where intuition, experience, and training combine without our being aware of it to produce a finished thought. A computer has only consciousness — or what passes for it. In order to instruct a computer, we must first have reasoned out exactly what we intend it to do.

None of our previous tools ever demanded that we examine and analyze the way we think to such a high degree, and for us this is a new and not very comfortable experience. Before the Computer Age, it was easier to overlook inconsistencies in our ideas and to compartmentalize our thoughts so as to ignore the contradictions among them, by and large. Some call it hypocrisy; others accept it as convenience, or the price to be paid for living in the world. Many, if not most of us, become so adept at maneuvering around the conflicts in our thinking that we never even pay attention to them.

Programming, however, is not only an abstraction of our ways of thinking; it is a reflection of them. We may, like the Red Queen of *Alice in Wonderland*, be able to believe six impossible things before breakfast, but trying to get the computer to obey contradictory instructions is worse than an exercise in futility. It can cause real damage, as previous chapters have discussed. Programs cannot tolerate sloppiness. To be a successful programmer means training oneself in the disciplines of logic, recognizing that contradictions must be overcome and inconsistencies resolved; it means one must understand that what other people will let slide by is not acceptable to a computer. Good programmers are often not easy people to live with.

Programming reflects our patterns of thinking in other ways as well. One of the fastest growing uses of the computer is for playing games, which are becoming ever more complex expressions of our fantasies. On the other hand, the even faster growing collection of databases about our personal lives also feeds our appetite for gossip. And nasty little children (of whatever chronological age) who in a more innocent era might have amused themselves by throwing rocks at passing cars now find the creation of computer viruses a much more satisfying outlet for their destructive impulses.

The computer, our most excellent and obedient servant, is willing to play any role we are clever enough to explain to it, with no compunctions whatever. There is no ethical circuit board, and no safeguard against a programmer's mischief except that which another programmer remembers to devise. If we are uneasy about our creation, it is with reason; more than any other tool of our devising, the computer comes closest to mimicking our conscious thoughts. It is a mirror that, however distorted, sometimes shows us a side of ourselves we would rather not have seen.

But live with it we must. Our lives are already so intertwined with this new creation of ours that there is no way we can give it up. The way we work and play, the way we shop, our access to our money and to health services, the cars we drive, at times even our very heartbeats — all are guided and even controlled by some programmer's thoughts encased in a silicon chip. As the mythologies of the past have taught us, there is no going back to a more innocent time. There is no closing of Pandora's box, no putting the apple back on the tree.

And if the knowledge of good and evil is a sword that, once drawn, cannot be resheathed, so it is with the computer. Our awareness of its potential both to help and to harm, and our understanding of its limitations as well as its strengths, must guide us in the proper use of this most powerful and difficult of tools. It may yet become a reflection — and a magnification — of the best that is within us.

Appendix

NUMBER REPRESENTATIONS

I. POWERS OF 2 AND THEIR USES

Decimal values for the first 32 powers of 2:

2^0	1	2^1	2
2^2	4	2^3	8
2^4	16	2^5	32
2^6	64	2^7	128
2^8	256	2^9	512
2^{10}	1,024	2^{11}	2,048
2^{12}	4,096	2^{13}	8,192
2^{14}	16,384	2^{15}	32,768
2^{16}	65,536	2^{17}	131,072
2^{18}	262,144	2^{19}	524,288
2^{20}	1,048,576	2^{21}	2,097,152
2^{22}	4,194,304	2^{23}	8,388,608
2^{24}	16,777,216	2^{25}	33,554,432
2^{26}	67,108,864	2^{27}	134,217,728
2^{28}	268,435,456	2^{29}	536,870,912
2^{30}	1,073,741,824	2^{31}	2,147,483,648
2^{32}	4,294,967,296		

Each exponent represents the number of binary bits from the right (low-order) end of the binary number. Thus, 2^{13} in binary is:

0010 0000 0000 0000

which is the thirteenth bit, counting from the right end and starting at zero.

Certain of these numbers have acquired special significance in computer programming and design:

2^4 (16) There are sixteen numbers in the hexadecimal set. (See below.) Binary numbers are described in groups of four.

2^6 (64) Groups of six bits are no longer as common as they used to be, but there are still occasions where a collection of up to sixty-four items is useful.

2^7 (128) The lowest negative number in a signed byte is -128, while 127 (128–1) is the highest positive number. There are 128 characters in the basic ASCII set. Occasionally it is the size of a disk sector.

2^8 (256) This is the number of possible values in a byte, whose largest unsigned value is 255.

2^9 (512) This is the most common size of a disk sector on many computers.

2^{15} (32,768) The lowest negative number in a [16-bit] word is $-32,768$, while the highest positive number is 32,767.

2^{16} (65,536) This is the number of possible values in a word; also the highest unsigned number is 65,535. On some of the first PCs, this was the maximum size of memory.

2^{24} (16,777,216) On some machines, this is the maximum size of memory available to a single program.

2^{31} (2,147,483,648) This is the lowest negative number in a longword ($-2.147 \cdot 10^9$). The highest positive number in a longword is 2,147,483,647.

2^{32} (4,294,967,296) is the number of possible values in a longword, and is the maximum size of memory available to a single program on the largest machines.

II. HEXADECIMAL NUMBERS

Binary numbers are almost without exception represented as hexadecimal (hex) digits.

HEX	BINARY	DECIMAL		HEX	BINARY	DECIMAL
0	0000	0		1	0001	1
2	0010	2		3	0011	3
4	0100	4		5	0101	5
6	0110	6		7	0111	7
8	1000	8		9	1001	9
A	1010	10		B	1011	11
C	1100	12		D	1101	13
E	1110	14		F	1111	15

In this appendix, hex numbers are designated by a $_{16}$ subscript.

III. THE ASCII CHARACTER SET

The ASCII (American Standard Code for Information Interchange) character set has become the general industry standard. Almost all character I/O devices (keyboards, monitors, printers) process ASCII characters, although some mainframes still use EBCDIC.[†] Almost all text-mode telecommunications are done in ASCII. Standard ASCII characters fit into a byte; the first 128 character definitions are universally accepted, while the remaining 128 numbers (128–255) are called extended ASCII, and will vary from computer to computer.

The first thirty-two (20_{16}) characters are used for printing and transmission control. Many of them can be input from the keyboard as control characters by holding down the CTRL key and pressing the appropriate letter. Control characters are often described in computer literature with the up-arrow ($\wedge$A) or as CTRL-A.

DEC	HEX	NAME	COMMENTS
00	00	NUL	($\wedge$@) Often used as the end-of-string marker
01	01	SOH	($\wedge$A) Start of header; used in tele-communications
02	02	STX	($\wedge$B) Start of text (communications)
03	03	ETX	($\wedge$C) End of text; used in many systems to interrupt a program
04	04	EOT	($\wedge$D) End of transmission
05	05	ENQ	($\wedge$E) Enquiry
06	06	ACK	($\wedge$F) Acknowledge
07	07	BEL	($\wedge$G) Bell; audible alarm on terminal

[†]EBCDIC (Extended Binary Code Decimal Interchange Code) was invented by IBM for use with its System/360 computers and introduced in 1964. IBM still uses EBCDIC for its mainframe and midrange computers, although IBM-style PCs use ASCII. The most important difference between the two sets from a programming perspective is that in EBCDIC the order is lowercase letters, uppercase letters, and numbers. In ASCII, the order is different: numbers, uppercase letters, and lowercase letters. A program that conducts an alphanumeric sort must therefore take into account what kind of computer it is running on.

DEC	HEX	NAME	COMMENTS
08	08	BS	(∧H) Backspace — move the cursor or print head back one character; it does not automatically erase the character
09	09	HT	(∧I) Horizontal tab
10	0A	LF	(∧J) Line feed; moves the cursor down one line, staying in the same column
11	0B	VT	(∧K) Vertical tab; works mostly on hardcopy terminals
12	0C	FF	(∧L) Form feed; moves printer to top of next page. On screen, usually converted to four or more line feeds
13	0D	CR	(∧M) Carriage return. Returns the cursor or print head to the left margin; it does not advance the paper or move the cursor to the next line. The standard new-line combination is CR LF
14	0E	SO	(∧N) Shift out
15	0F	SI	(∧O) Shift in
16	10	DLE	(∧P) Data link escape
17	11	DC1	(∧Q) On many systems, this resumes the terminal output; see ∧S
18	12	DC2	(∧R) Device control 2
19	13	DC3	(∧S) On many systems, stop (hold) terminal output until ∧Q is entered
20	14	DC4	(∧T) Device control 4
21	15	NAK	(∧U) Negative acknowledge

DEC	HEX	NAME	COMMENTS
22	16	SYN	(∧V) Synchronous idle
23	17	ETB	(∧W) End of transmission block
24	18	CAN	(∧X) Cancel
25	19	EM	(∧Y) End of medium; on many interactive systems, ∧Y is also used to interrupt a running program
26	1A	SUB	(∧Z) Substitution; PC-DOS and other systems use this as an END-OF-FILE marker
27	1B	ESC	Escape. This character is often used on terminal or printer output, followed by a string of other characters, to perform special actions. These sequences are usually specific to the particular device. For example, on DEC's VT220 terminal, the output string $^{E}S_{C}20;24H$ will position the cursor to row 20, column 24
28	1C	FS	Figures shift
29	1D	GS	Group separator
30	1E	RS	Record separator
31	1F	US	Unit separator

Codes 32 through 176 are printable characters. Codes 32 through 47 are punctuation marks:

<SP>	32 (20_{16})	!	33 (21_{16})	"	34 (22_{16})	#	35 (23_{16})
$	36 (24_{16})	%	37 (25_{16})	&	38 (26_{16})	'	39 (27_{16})
(	40 (28_{16})	)	41 (29_{16})	*	42 ($2A_{16}$)	+	43 ($2B_{16}$)
'	44 ($2C_{16}$)	–	45 ($2D_{16}$)	.	46 ($2E_{16}$)	/	47 ($2F_{16}$)

("<SP>" means the "space" or "blank" character.)

The codes 48 through 57 (30_{16}–39_{16}) are the decimal numbers. They are arranged this way so that subtracting 30_{16} from the character will convert it to the binary number that the character represents.

0	48 (30_{16})	1	49 (31_{16})	2	50 (32_{16})	3	51 (33_{16})
4	52 (34_{16})	5	53 (35_{16})	6	54 (36_{16})	7	55 (37_{16})
8	56 (38_{16})	9	57 (39_{16})				

Codes 58 through 64 are more punctuation characters.

:	58 ($3A_{16}$)	;	59 ($3B_{16}$)	<	60 ($3C_{16}$)	=	61 ($3D_{16}$)
>	62 ($3E_{16}$)	?	63 ($3F_{16}$)	@	64 (40_{16})		

Codes 65 through 90 are the uppercase alphabetic characters. They are exactly 32 (20_{16}) less than their corresponding lowercase characters.

A	65 (41_{16})	B	66 (42_{16})	C	67 (43_{16})	D	68 (44_{16})
E	69 (45_{16})	F	70 (46_{16})	G	71 (47_{16})	H	72 (48_{16})
I	73 (49_{16})	J	74 ($4A_{16}$)	K	75 ($4B_{16}$)	L	76 ($4C_{16}$)
M	77 ($4D_{16}$)	N	78 ($4E_{16}$)	O	79 ($4F_{16}$)	P	80 (50_{16})
Q	81 (51_{16})	R	82 (52_{16})	S	83 (53_{16})	T	84 (54_{16})
U	85 (55_{16})	V	86 (56_{16})	W	87 (57_{16})	X	88 (58_{16})
Y	89 (59_{16})	Z	90 ($5A_{16}$)				

Codes 91 through 96 are more punctuation characters.

[	91 ($5B_{16}$)	\	92 ($5C_{16}$)	]	93 ($5D_{16}$)	^	94 ($5E_{16}$)
_	95 ($5F_{16}$)	´	96 (60_{16})				

Codes 97 through 122 are the lowercase alphabetics. They can be converted to uppercase by subtracting 32 (20_{16}), or by clearing bit 5 (20_{16}) of the character.

a 97 (61_{16}) b 98 (62_{16}) c 99 (63_{16}) d 100 (64_{16})

e 101 (65_{16}) f 102 (66_{16}) g 103 (67_{16}) h 104 (68_{16})

i 105 (69_{16}) j 106 $(6A_{16})$ k 107 $(6B_{16})$ l 108 $(6C_{16})$

m 109 $(6D_{16})$ n 110 $(6E_{16})$ o 111 $(6F_{16})$ p 112 (70_{16})

q 113 (71_{16}) r 114 (72_{16}) s 115 (73_{16}) t 116 (74_{16})

ü 117 (75_{16}) v 118 (76_{16}) w 119 (77_{16}) x 120 (78_{16})

y 121 (79_{16}) z 122 $(7A_{16})$

Codes 123 through 126 are the remaining punctuation characters.

{   123 $(7B_{16})$ | 124 $(7C_{16})$ }   125 $(7D_{16})$ ˜ 126 $(7E_{16})$

Code 127 $(7F_{16})$ is the DEL key on some systems. On others, it is a small solid box or a triangle ("◻"), and 255 (FF_{16}) is the DEL key. How the DEL key operates (backspace, backspace and erase) will depend on the particular operating system.

There is less agreement on the meaning of the codes between 128 and 255 — a range often called "extended ASCII." Characters are found here that appear in other Latin alphabets but are not found in English, such as Ñ (decimal 209), and symbols such as § (decimal 167). But even this extended range does not begin to cover the letters of the Cyrillic alphabet or Devanagari script (used by several languages of India), to say nothing of ideographic languages such as Chinese and Japanese. A number of different approaches are being taken to solve this problem, all of which involve using additional bytes to compose the characters. One such solution, developed by the Unicode Consortium, uses a word (two bytes) for each character, which allows for 65,536 possibilities. At last report, the Unicode Standard includes just under 40,000 characters, which allows it to encompass most of the principal written languages of the world.

Another approach that uses two bytes in sequence rather than as one word is to have the first byte designate a specific character set, while the second is the character within the set. The first byte should use a value greater than 128, so that these special characters can be intermingled with standard ASCII text. Again, there is no generally recognized standard yet for these extensions.

Character strings are even more fluid in representation because most computers do not have instructions that will operate on a string of characters directly, but require some prior instruction to set the parameters. In particular, the length of the string is subject to language design as well as to variations in the circuitry. The most common forms of string representation are:

- String with terminating character. In this form, the string is defined by its starting address and a terminating character, generally a null (binary 00000000) at the end. The C language is particularly partial to this form.
- Counted string. The address of the string is the address of a byte or word containing the number of characters (bytes) that follow.
- String descriptor. In this form, the address of a string is really the address of a descriptor. The first word or word part of the descriptor is the length of the string, while the address part of the descriptor is the address of the first character (byte) of the text of the string. Where the descriptor is two longwords (for a 32-bit address and a 16-bit byte count), the remaining 16 bits are either ignored or are used to describe special types of strings and other arrays.

IV. NUMBERS

Numbers in memory are always a set of binary bits grouped together as a byte (8 bits), a word (16 bits), a longword (32 bits), and sometimes in still larger groupings such as a quadword (64 bits). How these are used for numbers is strictly a function of the machine instructions that operate on them.

1. Unsigned Integers

Integers are whole numbers such as 1, 15, 65, 535. An unsigned integer is the same as an absolute number, which is always positive; therefore, all of the bits are used for the number value. Thus, standard memory groupings hold unsigned integers in these ranges:

Byte (8 bits)	0–255
Word (16 bits)	0–65,535
Longword (32 bits)	0–4,294,967,295

2. Signed Integers

In a signed integer, one bit—the leftmost—is used to represent the sign, which by long-standing convention is 0 for (+) and 1 for (−). The remaining bits are used for the number value. Ranges for standard sizes are:

Byte (7 bits plus sign)	−128 − +127
Word (15 bits plus sign)	−32,768 − +32,767
Longword (31 bits plus sign)	−2,147,483,648 − +2,147,483,647

Negative numbers use "two's-complement" notation, which allows for more efficient arithmetic logic. Two's complement works by taking the complement (the opposite number) of each binary bit and then adding 1 to the resulting number. For example, the decimal number 54 is 00110110 in binary (as held in a byte). The byte value for -54 is calculated as:

$$00110110 \rightarrow \text{one's complement: } 11001001$$
$$+1$$
$$\overline{}$$
$$\rightarrow \text{two's complement: } 11001010$$

(This operation also automatically sets the sign bit to '1'.)

3. Real Numbers

Real numbers, or floating point numbers, are always signed, and their representation will be different on different machines, according to the manufacturer's design. But while FORTRAN and other high-level language compilers will handle the details of constructing and using floating point numbers, their structure dictates certain restrictions that should be kept in mind.

Floating point numbers are derived from scientific notation. For example, 1,537 can be written in scientific notation as

$$.1537 \cdot 10^4.$$

where the "4" is the exponent and the "1537" is the fraction. In a computer representation, a certain number of bits in a longword are set aside for a binary exponent (also called the characteristic), one bit for the sign, and the remainder are set aside for the fraction (sometimes designated the *mantissa*). The exponent represents binary powers of 2 (either positive or negative), and the fraction is the number itself.[†] A 32-bit longword divided up as:

Sign   1 bit
Exponent   8 bits
Fraction   23 bits

can hold real numbers in the approximate range $\pm.3 \cdot 10^{-38}$ to $\pm 2 \cdot 10^{38}$. Other arrangements of the parts of the floating point number will allow for either larger and smaller numbers (by giving more bits to the exponent) or for greater precision—more numbers to the right of the decimal point—by increasing the number of bits given to the fraction. A 128-bit octaword with a 15-bit exponent can hold a number as high as 10^{4932}, with 33 digits to the right of the decimal point.

4. Variable-length Numbers

It is possible to represent numbers in an indefinite length format where the number of digits or bytes is specified at the start or end of the string. These types of numbers are often called packed decimal (another form is zoned decimal), and are used primarily in business applications where large numbers with small precision (places to the right of the decimal point) are needed. Billions or even trillions of dollars may be involved, but each figure has at most ninety-nine cents, so two digits of precision are enough. COBOL in particular converts most of its internal data storage into packed decimal, so the COBOL programmer is not generally required to take notice of the internal structure. An assembly language programmer working in packed decimal should refer to the appropriate language manual, since representations may vary.

[†]Details of how the exponent is actually represented vary from machine to machine; see a specific manufacturer's literature for the details.

Acknowledgments

Writing is, as they say, a solitary business, but in reality there is a community of support hovering just behind the author's shoulder, without which we could never hope to succeed. Heidi Seifert, Ron and Pat Kastner, Jay Azneer, Mark Chimsky and Rob Lustig, John and Jobyna Dellar, Jo Leggett, and Eric Hansen were among those whose enthusiasm for this project helped me to see it through. My colleagues at the Bank of America have been generous with their knowledge. My family's encouragement helped me see beyond the dark moments of silence that plague every writer. I appreciate as well the supreme confidence that my editor, Bob Weil, displayed as he casually suggested I should rewrite this and change that—which led me to rewrite the entire book by the time I was done. His assistant, Andrew Miller, proved invaluable as a line editor, and Naomi Shulman was an excellent production editor. I am also grateful for the help and advice I received from Peggy Kidwell at the Smithsonian and Dag Spicer of The Computer Museum, and for the drawings made by Doug

Smith of DMS Comunication Design. Most of all, this book owes a debt to Jean Marcucci for the endless evenings spent patiently waiting for me to finish just one more page, to touch up just one more line, and for reading chapter after chapter just one more time.

DANIEL KOHANSKI
San Francisco, California

Glossary

abort   The abnormal termination of a program.

absolute number   See *number, unsigned.*

address   In memory, the location of a particular byte. For disk or tape, the number of a particular block or sector.

address space   The area of memory available to the running program. Most programs (except the operating system) do not have access to all of the memory. In some cases, a program can arrange through operating system service calls to have access to different parts of memory at different times.

algorithm   A precisely defined set of actions taken to solve a problem.

application program   A program that performs a specific task or set of tasks in coordination with an operating system. The task may be anything from a calculator to a word processor to a database management program.

argument   See *parameter.*

ARPAnet   A loosely organized research network of university, government and corporate computer systems that used a common communications protocol, funded by the Defense Advanced Research Projects Agency (DARPA, later ARPA). The ARPAnet has evolved into the Internet.

array   An ordered arrangement of units of data; a collection of scalars. Arrays are manipulated one unit at a time by using an index; other times the address of the first unit is used to refer to the array as a whole. An array can be organized into any number of dimensions, limited only by the capacity of memory and the limitations of the language. An array of more than one dimension is often called a matrix.

artificial intelligence   The ability of computers to reason in a manner similar to human beings. It is still largely a theoretical study.

ASCII   American Standard Code for Information Interchange (pronounced "ASK-ee"). It is the set of binary representations of the standard characters (A-Z, a-z, etc.) that most computers and peripherals use. Compare to *EBCDIC*.

assembler   A program that converts assembly language source code to machine language.

assembly language   The symbolic equivalent of machine language, using meaningful mnemonics (e.g., READ, LOAD, STORE) to represent binary machine instructions. In general, one instruction in assembly language converts into one machine language instruction.

assignment statement   A statement that performs an operation on one or more operands and stores the result in a specified location.

asynchronous I/O   An input or output (I/O) operation that, once started, operates indepedently of the starting program. Contrast with synchronous I/O.

backwards compatibility   A quality of a new version of a language, operating system, or hardware such that programs that used to work under the previous version will also work with this one.

backup A copy of source and other files on some removable storage medium, such as a disk or tape.

batch processing A method of executing programs under the control of the operating system in isolation from a human user.

begin-end pair The pair of keywords which mark the start and end of a code block in a high-level language.

binary numbers A two-digit number system (zero and one). Ultimately, all data in memory consists of binary numbers (circuits which are either ON [1] or OFF [0]).

binary operator An operator which requires two operands.

bit The smallest unit of memory, always zero or one.

block (code) A section of structured code which is isolated from other parts of the program, so that its entry and exit are controlled. Local variables declared within the block cannot be accessed outside the block.

block (disk) The grouping of one or more disk file records into a unit that is read or written with one I/O operation. The size of the block is related to the physical characteristics of the I/O device.

block I/O Input from or output to a file or I/O device using groups of data. Contrast with record I/O.

boolean value See *logical value*.

boot A hardware operation that takes the computer from the "power on" state to a usable condition. Its major function is to locate and read in the operating system.

break A control statement which causes the program to break out of the current if-then-else, do-while, or switch construction.

breakpoint A software trap set by the debugger in the running program. When the breakpoint is executed, it transfers control of the computer to the debugger.

buffer   A section of memory, usually defined as an array, that contains variable amount of data. The term is usually associated with I/O operations.

bug   An error in a program (colloquial).

byte   The smallest addressable unit of memory. It almost always consists of eight bits.

C   A structured language, developed by Bell Labs in the early 1980s, that is flexible enough to be used to write operating system code as well as application programs. C and its descendants (C++ and JAVA) are some of the most popular languages in use today.

call   An instruction that changes the program flow to another location while preserving the address of the instruction following the call. It is used to execute a subroutine, function, routine, or procedure. The return instruction changes the execution flow back to the instruction after the call.

call by reference   A parameter passed to a subroutine as an address. The subroutine uses indirect addressing or pointer manipulation to access the data. The subroutine can also use this location as a means of passing complex data back to the caller.

call by value   A parameter passed to a subroutine as a value. The subroutine can use this value in its internal calculations, but cannot alter the original data.

carriage return   A control character that moves the cursor back to the leftmost column on the screen, or the print head back to the left margin of the paper. Often abbreviated as CR. Usually combined with *line feed.*

cathode ray tube   Also called a CRT. A rarely used term for *monitor.*

central processing unit   Also called a CPU. The central circuitry which performs the individual software instructions. Includes circuits to locate data in memory. Also includes the internal registers.

character   A letter, digit, punctuation mark, or symbol that can be typed in from a keyboard, displayed on a monitor, or printed by the printer. Standard characters (see the ASCII list in the Appendix) do not need any special processing, but special characters might.

chip   An integrated circuit, the successor to discrete transistors and vacuum tubes. A CPU is made up of one or more chips, as are memory boards and most other components of a modern computer.

COBOL   COmmon Business-Oriented Language, one of the earliest and most popular high-level languages, dating from 1959. Statements in COBOL are designed to resemble English and are written in sentence form.

comment   A statement in English or another natural language that is part of the source code only, and which explains the actions of the nearby instructions. It is marked according to the syntax of the language so that it is not processed by the assembler or compiler.

compiler   A program that converts high-level language source code into machine language. Its output is an object file.

computer   A device, generally electronic, that stores information and the commands to process that information.

conditional branch   A change in the program flow that is taken only if some condition is TRUE.

conditional expression   A constant, variable, or operation which produces a logical value TRUE or FALSE. Used in control statements.

constant   A unit of memory whose contents are fixed in the source code, and which does not change during program execution. See also *literal*.

contiguous file   A disk file whose physical sector addresses are in exact sequential order with no gaps. All tape files are contiguous.

continue   A control statement that stops the current iteration of a do-while construction and proceeds to the next iteration.

control statement   A statement that changes the program flow based on the value of a conditional expression.

conversion   The act of changing one type of memory unit into another for purposes of performing an operation. For example, a word (16 bits) must be converted to a longword (32 bits) before its contents can be added to those of another longword. Similarly, an integer must be converted to a floating point number before it can be added to another floating point number.

core   An obsolete term for memory.

CPU   See *central processing unit*.

CRT   See *cathode ray tube*.

data space   The part of a program that contains variable data; it can be changed during program execution. Contrast with *program space*.

data transformation   A type of operation statement that manipulates (transforms) an element, or a group of elements, of data.

data transport   A type of operation statement that moves (transports) an element or set of elements of data from one location to another.

data type   The classification of a particular instance of data, such as integer, character, floating point.

database   An organized collection of data.

debugger   An special set of functions that, when linked together with a program, enables the programmer to monitor and modify the execution of that program.

default   Data that, if left out of some specification, will be assumed by the operating system, language, or program.

default directory   The current directory or subdirectory. In particular, if an operating system command or user program specifies a file by name and extension only, the operating system will look for that file in the default directory.

directory   A disk file whose contents are the file names and sector addresses of other files.

disk   A magnetic storage device attached to the computer. The disk is capable of storing large amounts of data, which is divided into sectors that can be accessed randomly — that is, the disk drive can access any new sector regardless of where it happens to be positioned at the moment. Data can include stored programs. Some disks are removable; others are a fixed combination of magnetic platter(s) and drive mechanism.

double floating point number   A floating point number contained in a unit of memory double the size of a standard floating point number. Usually a quadword (64 bits). See *floating point number*.

do-while   An iterative type of control statement that causes a block of code to be repeatedly executed until some condition is satisfied.

dump   A file or printout containing the binary contents of a program's data space at a particular moment — generally the moment the program failed. It is used as an aid to diagnosing problems.

EBCDIC   Extended Binary Coded Decimal Interchange Code. A set of binary representations of the standard character set. It was developed for the IBM 360 set of computers in the early

1960s, and is still used on many IBM computers, but most of the computer world now uses ASCII. EBCDIC differs from ASCII in that it uses values between 128 and 255 for most of its printable characters; contains more printer control codes; and puts lowercase letters first, followed by uppercase letters and then numbers.

editor   A program which allows the user to create and modify text files, including source programs.

element   A unit of data in an array.

embedded system   A special-purpose program built into a chip and used to control an appliance, such as a microwave or television set, or other devices, such as an automobile exhaust system.

encapsulation   A feature of object-oriented programming: it allows the programmer to hide the code and data structure of an object from other parts of the program.

entry point   The first instruction to be executed in the program.

end of file   An input condition indicating that the last piece of data has been read in from a data file.

EOF   See *end of file*.

ergonomics   The science of designing furniture, appliances, and especially computer programs for the comfort and convenience of the user.

escape sequence   A character string starting with the ESC character that performs a special operation on the terminal or printer.

executable file   A program in machine instruction form. When the operating system runs a program, it reads the executable file from disk into memory and transfers control of the CPU to the designated starting instruction. The most common extension for an executable file is EXE.

execution The use of a program. "Execute" and "run" are equivalent. Also, the performance of an instruction.

exit Returns complete control of the computer to the operating system. The action a program takes when it terminates normally (see *abort*).

expert system A program that emulates (or tries to emulate) the thought processes of a human expert, such as an engineer or physician.

extension The part of the filename to the right of the period. It usually serves to describe the file type; for example, the OBJ extension is used to describe an object file.

external reference A variable or function name that is not defined in the current code block. It must be resolved by the linker, using a global name in another module of the program or in an object library.

file A group of sectors on the disk that have been organized into an ordered collection of data and given a name (and usually an extension). See *directory*.

filename (1) The full name of a file in the form "xxxxxx.xxx." (2) The first part of the name of a file (the part to the left of the period).

floating point number A number with an integer part and a fractional part. Requires a longword or larger unit of memory.

for A specialized form of iterative loop based on a counter.

format A description of the form of an input or output string (numbers, floating point numbers, characters, etc.).

FORTRAN FORmula TRANslation. One of the oldest—and still popular—high-level languages, in which statements take a form similar to arithmetic formulas.

function The basic coding unit of structured programming. A function is entered via a CALL statement and exits by using a RETURN statement.

general purpose register   A register that is completely under program control. These registers are used to contain the results of arithmetic calculation, and are also used for index and indirect operations.

gigabyte   One billion bytes. Used on occasion to describe the size of memory and disks.

global variable   A variable name that is meaningful to all modules in the program.

goto   A control statement that unconditionally changes the execution flow. It is considered by some to be extremely dangerous because of its potential to create errors that are difficult to trace. Some languages do not permit its use.

hardware   A general term for the physical circuitry, boards, container, and other parts of the computer.

hex   See *hexadecimal*.

hexadecimal   A sixteen-digit number set equivalent to binary numbers in which each group of four binary numbers is represented as one hexadecimal digit. Usually abbreviated as "hex." The first ten digits are 0 (zero) through 9; the remaining digits are A through F.

high-level language   A computer language other than assembly language. Each instruction statement in a high-level language converts into one or more machine language instructions. High-level languages require a compiler to convert them to machine language. Many high-level languages are geared toward working with a particular class of problems (COBOL was designed for business applications, for example).

I/O   See *input/output*.

if-then-else   An alternative type of control statement. Depending on the resolution of the conditional (if), either the first part (then) or the second part (else) will be executed. The "else" part is usually optional.

index   The number of an element of an array. If the array has more than one dimension, each dimension has its own index.

indirect addressing   Access to a location in memory by using a pointer instead of the direct address.

infinite loop   A section of code that repeats itself indefinitely. This is a common type of program error (or *bug*).

inheritance   A feature of object-oriented languages that permits a programmer to describe code and data structures for one class of objects and then reassign them in whole or in part to another class of objects without redefining them.

initialization   The setting of an initial value into a unit of memory. All units always contain some value, but unless they are somehow initialized, these contents are random.

input/output   The means by which the computer communicates with the outside world; often called I/O. I/O devices include terminals (keyboard and monitor), disks, tapes, modems, and printers. The direction is always from the point of view of memory: input reads data *into* memory; output writes data *out* of memory to some device.

instruction   In machine language, a single command to the computer circuitry, such as "ADD" or "LOAD."

interactive processing   A technique for executing programs under the direct control of a user, generally via a terminal.

Internet   Successor to the ARPAnet, a global network of computers, including commercial providers, through which users may exchange data, documents, and other communications. Sometimes known as the "information superhighway."

interrupt   A hardware or software signal to the operating system that causes the system to suspend the current program and execute a special section of code.

JAVA   An object-oriented language developed by Sun Microsystems in the early 1990s with particular emphasis on portability and on ease of interaction with the Internet.

keyboard   An input device of a terminal consisting of one typewriter-style key for each alphabetic, numeric, and special character, plus extra function keys. Most keyboards now on the market have at least 101 keys, some of which may be duplicates.

keyword   A symbol or string of text characters which have a predefined meaning to the compiler or assembler. Generally, a keyword can be used only in accordance with the rules for that keyword.

label   The symbolic name of a location in memory.

language   A representation of instructions to the computer using words and phrases that more or less resemble English or other natural languages. See *assembler; high-level language.*

library   A disk file that contains functions in source or object form. Source library functions and code are included in the program by compiler statements. Object libraries are used by the linker.

line feed   A control character that moves the cursor down one row on the screen, or which advances the printer paper by one line. Often abbreviated as LF. Usually combined with *carriage return.*

linker   A program which converts one or more object files into an executable file. The link process includes resolving all symbolic references and incorporating modules from specified object libraries.

listing   A text printout generated by the compiler or assembler showing all the statements of the source program, including comments. If the compiler or assembler finds any errors in the source code, these will be included in the listing. All assemblers and some compilers will include the machine language output in the listing.

literal   A symbol used for its literal value.

local variable   A variable name that has meaning only within a single code block.

logical operator   An operator whose result is a logical value.

logical value   TRUE or FALSE. Internal representations of TRUE and FALSE will depend on the language or on established conventions.

longword   A unit of memory, usually consisting of two words or four bytes—thirty-two bits.

machine language   The binary set of instructions, which are actually executed by the CPU.

mainframe   A large computer system capable of processing massive quantities of data.

mass storage   A device that holds a large quantity of data, such as a disk or tape.

megabyte   One million bytes. Used to describe the size of memory or disk.

memory   Internal data storage. A CPU can operate directly on data only if it is in memory, and a program can run only while it is in memory. Memory is relatively small compared to disk space, and generally loses its contents when the power is turned off.

mercury delay line   An early memory unit designed to retain its setting (1 or 0) by propagating a sound wave through mercury.

MFLOPS   Million FLOating Point instructions per Second. See *MIPS*.

microcomputer   A small computer dedicated to a single use, generally as a personal computer.

minicomputer   A medium-size computer, often designed to move data quickly to and from terminals. Although minicomputers are sometimes as powerful as mainframes, they are not as oriented toward large-scale data processing.

MIPS   <u>M</u>illion <u>I</u>nstructions <u>P</u>er <u>S</u>econd. MIPS and MFLOPS are ways of measuring computer performance, usually in comparison with other CPUs.

mnemonic   The symbolic representation of a machine instruction code. On the VAX machine, for example, the mnemonic ADDL2 (add two longwords) represents the binary op code 11000000.

modem   An I/O device that connects a computer or a terminal to another computer by using a telephone circuit.

modular programming   An expansion of structured programming theory: a program is divided into separate modules, each of which performs one specific task for the program.

module   Generally, a set of procedures grouped together in one source code file.

modulo   (mod) The remainder of an integer division, expressed as an integer. The value of "17 mod 5" is 2.

monitor   A video display (CRT) resembling a TV screen, which is the output part of a terminal.

multiprogramming   The apparently simultaneous execution of more than one program on the same physical computer.

nesting   (1) The inclusion of a parenthetical operation inside another parenthetical. (2) The inclusion of a code block inside another code block.

number, signed   A number with a sign (+ or −). The high-order or leftmost bit of the data space is used for the sign, and the other bits are used for the number. A byte, for instance, can hold signed numbers in the range -128 through 0 to $+127$. See also *number, unsigned.*

number, unsigned   A number with no sign, and therefore in the range zero to the maximum value of the data type. In a byte, for example, unsigned numbers range from 0 to 255.

object   An organized set of data descriptions and the code that operates on them. It is the basic unit of object-oriented programming.

object file   The intermediate form of a program that has been converted from a source file by a compiler or assembler. One or more object files are linked together to form an executable file. The most common extension for an object file is OBJ.

object-oriented programming   An extension of structured programming in which the code is contained in an object which describes the data structures as well. The purpose of this method is to minimize the misuse of data and to facilitate the division of programming tasks among a group of programmers.

octaword   (rare) A unit of memory, eight words (sixteen bytes), or 128 bits.

one-based numbering   A method of accessing the elements of an array. In this approach, the first element of each dimension is accessed using an index value of 1. Contrast with *zero-based numbering.*

op code   A binary number contained in one or more bytes that the computer circuitry interprets as a machine instruction.

operand   A constant, variable, or function return value, which is the object of an operator.

operating system   The basic program that controls the computer, and which is always running in the background. It carries out the user's commands, schedules programs to run, and provides I/O and other services to the running program. On shared systems, it is also responsible for system integrity and for managing multiple simultaneous operations.

operator   A symbol that the compiler converts into a machine language instruction. An operator is always associated with one or more operands.

output   See *input/output*.

parallel processing   The simultaneous operation of different hardware circuits. It is possible to arrange several CPUs to operate in parallel, but it is proving extremely difficult to design programs that will use this type of organization efficiently.

parameter   A unit of data passed to a subroutine or function. See *call by value; call by reference*.

PASCAL   A structured programming language in use since the early 1970s.

path   The full description of a file. It includes the device name, the directory (and the subdirectories), the file name and the extension.

PC   See *personal computer*.

personal computer   Also called a PC. A computer that is small enough and (usually) cheap enough to be used by one person at home or as an office workstation.

platform   The combination of a specific computer and operating system.

pointer   A unit of memory that contains an address of some other unit of memory.

polymorphism   A feature of object-oriented programming that allows a programmer to extend an object definition by redefining some of its parts.

portability   The ability of a program to run unchanged on several different types of platforms.

precedence   The order in which operators are executed.

precision   Used in describing floating point numbers: the number of decimal digits in the fractional part that can be contained in the floating point unit. On most machines, a longword can hold up to six digits of a fraction, while a double floating point number (quadword) has fourteen digits of precision.

printer   An output-only device that prints character text and graphics on paper.

privileged operation   A machine instruction that can only be executed when the CPU is in a special state. The CPU state is under the control of the operating system, which normally restricts applications to the lowest, unprivileged state. Privileged instructions include the actual I/O commands and instructions to set up and expand program and data space.

procedure   A generic term for a section of code that is entered by a CALL and ends with RETURN. Usually refers to a substantial section of code performing a major task. Also called a *function* or *module*.

program   A set of instructions which, taken as a whole, cause the computer to perform a specific task.

program counter   The register that contains the address of the next instruction in memory which the CPU will execute.

program flow   The order of execution of the instructions of a program. Unless changed by a conditional or unconditional branch, after each instruction is executed, the next instruction after it is the next one executed. Also called an *execution flow*.

program space   The part of a program that contains the machine language instructions and constants. Its contents cannot be altered during program execution. Contrast with *data space*.

programmer   A person trained in one or more computer languages who uses those languages to create computer programs.

protocol   A set of conventions established by general or specific agreement to allow two computers to communicate with one another. Various protocols cover the layout of data files, the mechanics of data transmission, and so on.

prototype   A description of a function or routine, including the name, the data type of the return value, and (sometimes) the number and data types of the parameters. A prototype is required in some languages where the routine is called prior to its being defined.

quadword   A unit of memory, usually consisting of four words (eight bytes) or sixty-four bits.

random access   A method of reading or writing bytes in memory or sectors on the disk by accessing the location directly, regardless of the previous location accessed.

read   An input operation. This term is usually used with large amounts of data, such as one or more disk or tape sectors, but can also refer to a single character operation.

read-only   A file or a section of memory whose data can be accessed but not changed. Contrast with *writable*.

real number   See *floating point number*.

real-time processing   A specialized form of program execution in which the computer controls I/O devices that must function in coordination with external events, such as an automated factory assembly line.

record I/O   Input to or output from a file or I/O device using logical groups of data. The size of the record is related to the nature of the data, not to the physical device.

register   A special circuit in the CPU that contains volatile information, such as the address of the next instruction, or the location of the program stack. Most registers can be at least partially controlled by the program. The size of a register is usually the number of bits needed to hold a memory address. See also *general purpose register.*

relational operator   An operator which sets a logical value based on the relation (equal to, greater than, etc.) of the operands. Used in conditional expressions.

return   The last action of a subroutine, function, routine or procedure. It changes the program flow to the location following the most recent CALL instruction.

return value   A unit of data which is returned to the caller of a function; the value of a function.

root directory   The central directory of a disk.

round-off   Internal adjustment of floating point calculation yielding the closest approximation of the answer that will fit into the floating point number representation. See *precision.*

routine   A generic term for a separate section of code; generally, the code is entered by a call instruction, and exits with a return. Except for its use in the term *subroutine*, it has become rare.

scalar   A simple unit of data. Usually used in contrast with array.

scope   The section(s) of code where a variable or function name has meaning. See *global variable; local variable.*

screen   See *monitor.*

sector   The smallest addressable unit of data on the disk. Different manufacturers make disks of different sector sizes; common sizes are 128 and 512 bytes.

sequential access   A form of I/O operation. Access starts at the first segment of data, and proceeds in sequence through each successive segment. Tapes are the most common device that use this method.

serial processing   The execution of instructions in sequence. Contrast with *parallel processing.*

sharable   A description of a file or an area in memory which can be accessed simultaneously by more than one program.

sign bit   The leftmost bit of a data element; if 0, the number is positive, if 1, the number is negative. See *number, signed.*

software   The set of instructions that cause the computer to operate; a program or set of programs.

source code   A program in the form of statements written in some language that a human being can understand. A compiler or assembler will convert source code to object form, and the linker will combine one or more objects into an executable program.

source file   A disk file containing a program in its source code form. The extension part of the filename usually describes the language. Examples are CBL (COBOL), FOR (FORTRAN), MAR (assembler), and C (the C language).

source program   See *source code.*

stack   A section of memory with pointers, organized so as to contain the return address of a CALL instruction, as well as other data that needs to be temporarily preserved.

statement   A line or lines of text in a high-level or assembly language.

storage media   A generic term for disks and tapes; devices where data is stored until it is needed by the computer. The term most often refers to those disks and tapes that can be physically removed from the computer and stored elsewhere.

string   A sequential group of bytes; in particular, a group of bytes whose contents are valid text characters. The string is described by the address of the first byte, and some indicator of the end: a marker, a count of the bytes, or the address of the last byte.

strongly typed language   A language that does not allow different data types (words, floating point numbers) to be used in the same statement. See *conversion*.

structure   An organized set of different data elements, which need not be of the same type. A structure can be accessed all at once or piece by piece.

structured programming   A theory of programming in which the statements in a computer language enforce a tight coding discipline. Also includes *modular programming; object-oriented programming* expands on it.

subdirectory   A directory inside another directory. Ultimately, all directories on a disk are subdirectories of the root directory.

subroutine   A section of code that is called from any point in the program. After completing its task, it returns to the caller. Subroutines are functions, but the term is most often used to describe a function contained in the same source code module that performs a small task.

switch   A control statement that directs the execution flow to one of several statements depending on some value.

synchronous I/O   Input or output that is coordinated with the program. The program is suspended until the I/O operation completes. Contrast with *asynchronous I/O*.

syntax   The grammatical rules of a computer language.

system service   A service, such as input and output, provided by the operating system. It generally takes the form of a CALL or a special op code.

tape   A magnetic storage device in the form of a strip of tape. The data is divided into blocks of any length, and access is sequential. A tape is made available to the computer by mounting it on a tape drive.

template   A description of a complex set of data.

terabyte   One trillion bytes. Rare (for now).

terminal   The basic I/O device connecting the user to the computer. It consists of a keyboard and a monitor or hard-copy printer, and interfaces interactively with the operating system or an application program.

time-sharing   The division of the CPU resource among several programs. See *multiprogramming*.

transistor   A solid-state device that functions as an electronic switch, changing its setting between zero and one in response to some electronic signal. Invented in 1947, the transistor quickly replaced the vacuum tube as the major component of the computer. Modern integrated circuits (*chips*) consist of millions of transistors etched into a silicon surface.

trap   An interrupt signal to the operating system that a program has attempted to perform some illegal operation.

truncation   In the division of two integers, the exclusion of any fractional part.

unary operator   An operator that uses one and only one operand.

unconditional branch   A change in the program flow to some other location in the program.

vaporware   A program or other computer product that has not yet been created, but which someone — often a salesperson — pretends already exists.

vacuum tube   A major component of early computers, a vacuum tube can switch states between zero and one in response to an external signal.

variable   A location in memory whose contents can be changed in the course of program execution. Also, the symbolic name of a location in memory.

VDT   Video Display Terminal. Another (rare) word for *monitor*. See also *CRT*.

von Neumann machine   A description given to all computers in use today, since they are all serial processors running programs stored in memory. This is the design that John von Neumann proposed in the "First Draft of a Report on the EDVAC" computer, circulated (though never published) in 1945. There is an ongoing controversy among computer historians over how much credit von Neumann deserves for various aspects of the design.

word   A unit of memory, usually consisting of two bytes or sixteen bits.

word processor   A program that mimics a typewriter, with many features added, enabling a person to compose a document on a computer, preserve it in a disk file, and print it on a hard-copy printer.

writable   A file or section of memory whose contents can be altered as well as accessed. Contrast with Read-Only. The operating system controls this setting by means of privileged operations.

write   An output operation, sending data from memory to a screen, disk or tape file, or other output device.

year 2000 problem   A term covering a variety of potential programming problems that will manifest themselves as the year 2000 gets closer and ultimately comes to pass. The class of problems is the result of a common tendency to represent the calendar year as a two-digit field, making it impossible to tell that the year 2000 (represented as "00") is later than 1999 (represented as "99"). Also, some programs may not know that 2000 is a leap year.

zero-based numbering   A method of accessing the elements of an array. In this approach, the first element of each dimension is accessed by an index value of zero. Contrast with *one-based numbering*.

Selected
Bibliography

Association for Computing Machinery. "ACM Code of Ethics and Professional Conduct." *Communications of the ACM* 36, no. 2 (February 1993): 99–105.

Au, Edith, and Dave Makower. *JAVA Programming Basics.* New York: Henry Holt and Co., MIS: Press, 1996.

Backus, John. "The History of Fortran I, II, and III." In *History of Programming Languages,* edited by Richard L. Wexelblat. New York: Academic Press, 1981.

———. "Can Programming Be Liberated from the Von Neumann Style?" In *Programming Languages: A Grand Tour,* 2d ed., edited by Ellis Horowitz. Rockville, MD: Computer Science Press, 1987. First published in *Communications of the ACM* 21, no. 8 (1978): 613–41.

Brookshear, J. Glenn. *Computer Science: An Overview.* Reading, MA: Addison-Wesley, 1997.

Campbell-Kelly, Martin, and William Aspray. *Computer: A History of the Information Machine.* New York: BasicBooks, 1996.

Dahl, Ole-Johan, Edsger W. Dijkstra, and C. A. R. Hoare. *Structured Programming.* London: Academic Press, 1972.

Davis, Alan M. *201 Principles of Software Development*. New York: McGraw Hill, 1995.

Dijkstra, Edgser. "GoTo Statement Considered Harmful." In *Great Papers in Computer Science*, edited by Phillip Laplante. St. Paul: West Publishing, 1996. First published in *Communications of the ACM*, 11, no. 3 (1968): 147–48.

Ermann, M. David, Mary B. Williams, and Claudio Gutierrez, eds. *Computers, Ethics, and Society*. New York: Oxford University Press, 1990.

Forester, Tom, and Perry Morrison. *Computer Ethics*, 2d ed. Cambridge, MA: MIT Press, 1994.

Freedman, Alan. *The Computer Desktop Encyclopedia*. New York: American Management Association, 1996.

Goldstine, Herman H. *The Computer from Pascal to von Neumann*, 2d ed. Princeton: Princeton University Press, 1993.

Holub, Allen I. *Enough Rope to Shoot Yourself in the Foot*. New York: McGraw-Hill, 1995.

Hopper, Grace. "Keynote Address." In *History of Programming Languages*, edited by Richard L. Wexelblat. New York: Academic Press, 1981.

Inglis, Jim. *Cobol 85 for Programmers*. Chichester, England: John Wiley and Sons, 1989.

Jamsa, Kris. *The C Library*. Berkeley, CA: Osborne McGraw-Hill, 1985.

Jenkins, Richard A. *Supercomputers of Today and Tomorrow: The Parallel Processing Revolution*. Blue Ridge Summit, PA: Tab Books, 1986.

Kidwell, Peggy A., and Paul E. Ceruzzi. *Landmarks in Digital Computing*. Washington, DC: Smithsonian Institution, 1994.

Koenig, Andrew, and Barbara Moo. *Ruminations on C + +*. Reading, MA: Addison-Wesley, 1997.

Knuth, Donald E. The Remaining Troublespots in ALGOL 60. In *Programming Languages: A Grand Tour*, 2d ed., edited by Ellis Horowitz. Rockville, MD: Computer Science Press, 1987. First published in *Communications of the ACM* 10, no. 10 (1967): 611–17.

———. *The Art of Computer Progamming* vol. 1, *Fundamental Algorithms*, 2d ed. Reading, MA: Addison-Wesley, 1973.

Kosko, Bart. *Fuzzy Thinking: The New Science of Fuzzy Logic*. New York: Hyperion, 1993.

Landauer, Thomas K. *The Trouble with Computers*. Cambridge: MIT Press, 1995.

Lee, Leonard. *The Day The Phones Stopped*. New York: Donald I. Fine, 1991.

McNeill, Daniel, and Paul Freiberger. *Fuzzy Logic*. New York: Simon & Schuster, 1993.

Metropolis, N., and Gian-Carlo Rota, eds. *A New Era in Computation*. Cambridge, MA: MIT Press, 1992.

Moler, Cleve. "A Tale of Two Numbers." In *The MathWorks, Inc.* [database online]. Natick, MA, ca. 1994–[Posted 21 December 1994]. Available from http://www.mathworks.com, The Pentium Papers, as MOLER_6.TXT.

Naur, Peter, et. al. "Revised Report on the Algorithmic Language ALGOL 60." In *Great Papers in Computer Science*, edited by Phillip Laplante. St. Paul, MN: West Publishing, 1996. Originally published in *Communications of the ACM* 6, no. 1 (1963): 1–20.

Niemeyer, Patrick, and Joshua Peck. *Exploring Java*. Bonn: O'Reilly and Associates, 1996.

Ritchie, David. *The Computer Pioneers*. New York: Simon and Schuster, 1986.

Sammet, Jean. "The Early History of COBOL." In *History of*

Programming Languages, edited by Richard L. Wexelblat. New York: Academic Press, 1981.

Sasha, Dennis, and Cathy Lazere. *Out of Their Minds: The Lives and Discoveries of 15 Great Computer Scientists.* New York: Springer-Verlag, 1995.

Shneiderman, Ben. The Relationship Between COBOL and Computer Science. In *Programming Languages: A Grand Tour,* 2d ed., edited by Ellis Horowitz. Rockville, MD: Computer Science Press, 1987. First published in *Annals of the History of Computing* 7:1 (Oct. 1985).

Slater, Robert. *Portraits in Silicon.* Cambridge, MA: MIT Press, 1987.

Stern, Nancy. *From ENIAC to UNIVAC: An Appraisal of the Eckert-Mauchly Computers.* Bedford, MA: Digital Press, 1981.

Ulrich, William M., and Ian S. Hayes. *The Year 2000 Software Crisis: Challenge of the Century.* Upper Saddle River, NJ: Prentice-Hall, 1997.

van der Linden, Peter. *Not Just Java.* Upper Saddle River, NJ: Prentice-Hall, 1997.

von Neumann, John. "First Draft of a Report on the EDVAC." [Unpublished document circulated in 1945 by Herman Goldstine.] Reprinted in full as an appendix in Stern (1981, 177–246).

Wegner, P. "Programming Languages — The First Twenty-five Years." In *Programming Languages: A Grand Tour,* 2d ed., edited by Ellis Horowitz. Rockville, MD: Computer Science Press, 1987. First published in *IEEE Transactions on Computers* (Dec. 1976): 1207–25.

A b o u t   t h e   A u t h o r

Daniel Kohanski was born in 1951, the same year that the first UNIVAC was delivered. He discovered computers in 1968 while pursuing a philosophy degree at Colgate University, and has been programming them ever since, along the way picking up a master's degree in computer science from Rutgers University in 1975. He has installed and maintained telecommunications systems in various odd corners of the world, a task that he describes as "performing neurosurgery without anaesthesia while the patient's relatives stand around and kibitz." Now he is a Consulting Systems Engineer for the Bank of America, and lives in San Francisco.